365 Easy One-Dish Recipes

Easy One-Dish Recipes for Everyday Family Meals

Cookbook Resources LLC
Highland Village, Texas

365 Easy One-Dish Recipes
Easy One-Dish Recipes for Everyday Family Meals

1st Printing - March 2008
2nd Printing - December 2008

International Standard Book Number: 978-1-59769-030-0

Library of Congress Number: 2008008963

Library of Congress Cataloging-in-Publication Data

    365 easy one-dish recipes : easy one-dish recipes for everyday family meals.
        p. cm.
     Includes index.
     ISBN 978-1-59769-030-0
     1. One-dish meals. 2. Quick and easy cookery. I. Cookbook Resources, LLC. II. Title: Three hundred sixty-five easy one-dish recipes.
     TX840.O53A145 2008
     641.8'2--dc22
                        2008008963

Cover by Nancy Bohanan

Edited, Designed and Published in the United States of America by
Cookbook Resources, LLC
541 Doubletree Drive
Highland Village, Texas 75077

Toll free 866-229-2665

www.cookbookresources.com

Bringing Family and Friends to the Table

365 Easy
One-Dish Recipes

365 Easy One-Dish Recipes is all about helping everyone who cooks do it in less time and really enjoy the results.

The importance of family meals is well known. Family meals do much to keep families together, to enrich lives and to instill healthy values and habits.

365 Easy One-Dish Recipes makes it easy to plan, to cook and to serve delicious dishes to family and friends. All the ingredients are readily available in your own pantry, refrigerator or the familiar shelves in your regular grocery store. Meals are easy when you start with easy recipes and an easy plan.

Most recipes do not need anything to go with them. Others are even better with a "bag salad" and bread from your own refrigerator or the grocery store. And there is a BONUS section in this book with desserts!

Do your part to enrich the lives of people around you. Serve a homecooked meal today!

Contents

Contents

Dedication

With a mission of helping you bring family and friends to the table, Cookbook Resources strives to make family meals and entertaining friends simple, easy and delicious.

We recognize the importance of a meal together as a means of building family bonds with memories and traditions that will be treasured for a lifetime. It is an opportunity to sit down with each other and share more than food.

This cookbook is dedicated with gratitude and respect for all those who show their love with homecooked meals, bringing family and friends to the table.

More and more statistical studies are finding that family meals play a significant role in childhood development. Children who eat with their families four or more nights per week are healthier, make better grades, score higher on aptitude tests and are less likely to have problems with drugs.

Beautiful Brunches

Casseroles, Breakfast Sandwiches, Coffee Cakes and French Toast

Beautiful Brunches Contents

Breakfast Frittata

2 medium zucchini, diced,
   drained
1 cup finely diced fresh
   mushrooms   70 g
Canola oil
2 ripe avocados, peeled, cubed
5 eggs
1½ cups shredded Swiss
   cheese   160 g

- Cook zucchini and mushrooms in large skillet with a little oil over medium heat for 4 to 5 minutes or just until tender. Remove from heat and sprinkle with a little salt and pepper.

- Place cubed avocado over top of vegetable mixture. Beat eggs and about 1 cup (250 ml) water or milk until frothy and pour over ingredients in skillet.

- Return skillet to medium heat, cover and cook for 5 minutes or until eggs set. Top with cheese, cover and cook for additional 1 minute or just until cheese melts. Cut in wedges to serve. Serves 6.

Corned Beef Hash-n-Eggs

1 (15 ounce) can corned
   beef hash   425 g
1 (11 ounce) can
   Mexicorn®, drained   310 g
4 eggs
¾ cup chili sauce   205 g

- Preheat oven to 375° (190° C).

- Spread corned beef hash in sprayed 9-inch (23 cm) pie pan and spoon corn over hash.

- With large spoon, make 4 depressions in corn and break 1 egg in each depression. Spoon chili sauce over top of eggs.

- Bake for 20 minutes or until eggs set. Serves 4.

Bacon & Eggs Anyone?

2 potatoes, peeled, cubed
¼ cup (½ stick) plus
   3 tablespoons butter,
     melted   90 g
¼ cup flour   30 g
1 (1 pint) carton
   half-and-half cream   455 g
1 (16 ounce) package
   shredded cheddar
   cheese   455 g
1 teaspoon dried
   Italian seasoning   5 ml
12 eggs, hard-boiled,
   sliced
1 pound bacon, cooked,
   slightly crumbled   455 g
1½ cups breadcrumbs 90 g

- Cook potatoes in salted water in saucepan just until tender, but do not overcook. Drain well.

- In separate saucepan, melt ¼ cup (60 g) butter and stir in flour. Cook, stirring constantly, 1 minute or until smooth.

- Gradually add half-and-half cream and cook over medium heat, stirring constantly, until sauce thickens. Add cheddar cheese, Italian seasoning, and a little salt and white pepper, stirring constantly, until cheese melts. Remove from heat.

- Layer half egg slices, half bacon and half cheese sauce in sprayed 9 x 13-inch (23 x 33 cm) baking dish. Spoon potatoes over cheese sauce and top with remaining egg slices, bacon and cheese sauce.

- Combine breadcrumbs and 3 tablespoons (45 ml) melted butter in bowl. Sprinkle over top of casserole. Cover and refrigerate overnight.

- When ready to bake, preheat oven to 350° (175° C).

- Before baking, remove casserole from refrigerator and let stand for about 20 minutes. Uncover and bake for 30 minutes. Serves 8 to 10.

Breakfast Bake

This is a favorite of ours for overnight guests or special enough for Christmas morning.

1 pound hot sausage,
   cooked, crumbled   455 g
1 cup shredded cheddar
   cheese   115 g
1 cup biscuit mix   120 g
5 eggs, slightly beaten
2 cups milk   500 ml

- Preheat oven to 350° (175° C).

- Place cooked, crumbled sausage in sprayed 9 x 13-inch (23 x 33 cm) baking dish and sprinkle with cheese.

- Combine biscuit mix, a little salt and eggs in bowl and beat well. Add milk and stir until fairly smooth. Pour over sausage mixture.

- Bake for 35 minutes. You can mix this up the night before cooking and refrigerate. To cook the next morning, add 5 minutes to cooking time. Serves 6.

Crabmeat Quiche

3 eggs, beaten
1 (8 ounce) carton sour
   cream   230 g
1 (6 ounce) can crabmeat,
   rinsed, drained, flaked 170 g
½ cup shredded Swiss
   cheese   115 g
1 (9 inch) piecrust   23 cm

- Preheat oven to 350° (175° C).

- Combine eggs and sour cream in bowl. Blend in crabmeat and cheese and add a little garlic salt and pepper.

- Pour into piecrust.

- Bake for 35 minutes. Serves 6.

Fiesta Eggs

1 pound sausage	455 g
½ green bell pepper, chopped	
½ red bell pepper, chopped	
3 green onions, chopped	
1 (10 ounce) can tomatoes and green chilies	280 g
½ cup hot, chunky salsa	130 g
½ cup cubed Velveeta® cheese	65 g
10 eggs, slightly beaten	
½ cup sour cream	120 g
⅔ cup milk	150 ml

- Preheat oven to 325° (160° C).

- Slowly brown sausage, bell peppers and onions in skillet. Spoon sausage-onion mixture onto paper towels, drain and set aside.

- Dry skillet with more paper towels, pour tomatoes and green chilies, salsa and cheese in skillet and cook, stirring constantly, only until cheese melts. Remove from heat.

- Beat eggs, 1½ teaspoons (7 ml) salt, sour cream and milk in bowl and fold in sausage mixture and tomato-cheese mixture. Transfer to sprayed 7 x 11-inch (18 x 28 cm) baking dish.

- Bake for about 25 minutes or until center is set. Serves 8.

Chiffon Cheese Souffle

Wow! Is this ever good! It is light and fluffy, but still very rich.

**12 slices white bread with
    crusts trimmed**
**2 (5 ounce) jars sharp
    processed cheese
    spread, softened   2 (145 g)**
6 eggs, beaten
3 cups milk   750 ml
**¾ cup (1½ sticks)
    butter, melted   170 g**

- Cut each bread slice into 4 triangles. Place dab of cheese on each triangle and place triangles evenly in layers in sprayed 9 x 13-inch (23 x 33 cm) baking dish. (You could certainly make this in a souffle dish if you have one.)

- Combine eggs, milk, butter and a little salt and pepper in bowl. Pour over layers. Cover and refrigerate for 8 hours.

- Remove from refrigerator 10 to 15 minutes before baking.

- When ready to bake, preheat oven to 350° (175° C).

- Bake for 1 hour. Serves 8.

Breakfast Tortillas

¾ **cup chopped onion   120 g**
¼ **cup (½ stick) butter 60 g**
¼ **cup flour   30 g**
¾ **cup milk   175 ml**
1 (1 pint) half-and-
    half cream   455 g
1 (7 ounce) can
    chopped green
    chilies   200 g
10 eggs
3 avocados
8 (8 inch) flour
    tortillas   8 (20 cm)
1 (8 ounce) package
    shredded Monterey
    Jack cheese   230 g

- Preheat oven to 350° (175° C).

- Saute onion in butter in large skillet. Stir in flour, cook on low 1 minute and stir constantly. Add milk and cream, cook on medium heat and stir constantly until mixture thickens.

- Add green chilies and ½ to 1 teaspoon (2 ml) each of salt and pepper. Remove sauce from heat and set aside.

- In separate skillet, scramble eggs lightly and remove from heat.

- Mash avocados and sprinkle with a little salt in small bowl.

- Spread tortillas on counter and dip 2 tablespoons (30 ml) sauce, one-eighth of eggs and one-eighth of avocados on each tortilla. Roll and place seam-side down on sprayed 9 x 13-inch (23 x 33 cm) baking dish. Spoon remaining sauce over tortillas.

- Cover and bake for about 25 minutes or just until tortillas are hot and bubbly. Remove from oven, sprinkle cheese over top and return to oven for about 10 minutes. When serving, top each tortilla with a dab of salsa, if desired. Serves 8.

TIP: To remove tortillas from baking pan, always use a long, wide spatula with holes in it so that the tortillas do not break up.

English Muffin Breakfast Sandwich

6 eggs
1 (8 ounce) package
   precooked bacon
   slices, halved   230 g
6 English muffins,
   halved, toasted
6 cheese slices

- Scramble eggs in skillet over medium heat and stir often. Season according to taste.

- Heat bacon in microwave according to package directions. Spoon egg mixture onto bottom of muffin, add cheese slice, bacon and muffin top. Serves 6.

Mexican Breakfast Eggs

4 tablespoons butter   60 g
9 eggs
3 tablespoons milk   45 ml
5 tablespoons salsa   75 g
1 cup crushed tortilla
   chips   55 g

- Melt butter in skillet. Beat eggs in bowl and add milk and salsa.

- Pour into skillet and stir until eggs are lightly cooked.

- Stir in tortilla chips and serve hot. Serves 6.

Quick Breakfast Sandwiches

*Wouldn't the kids love to say
they had sandwiches for
breakfast! What a cool Mom!*

8 slices white bread*
Butter, softened
**2 cups cooked, finely
   chopped ham**   **280 g**
**1 cup shredded Swiss
   cheese**   **110 g**
3 eggs, beaten
1⅔ cups milk   **400 ml**
**1 tablespoon minced
   onion flakes**   **15 ml**
1 teaspoon mustard   **5 ml**

- Trim crusts off bread slices. Spread butter on 1 side of each slice of bread. Place 4 slices in sprayed 8-inch (20 cm) square baking pan.

- Top bread slices with chopped ham and remaining bread slices, buttered-side up. Sprinkle with shredded Swiss cheese

- Combine eggs, milk, onion flakes, mustard and about ½ teaspoon (2 ml) salt in bowl and mix well. Slowly pour over bread slices. Cover and refrigerate overnight or at least 8 hours.

- When ready to bake, preheat oven to 325° (160° C).

- Remove baking pan from refrigerator about 10 minutes before cooking. Bake for 30 minutes or until center sets. To serve, cut into 4 sandwiches. Serves 4.

*TIP: Use regular bread slices, not thin sandwich slices.

Sunrise Eggs

6 eggs
2 cups milk   500 ml
1 pound sausage, cooked,
    browned   455 g
¾ cup shredded Velveeta®
    cheese   85 g
6 slices white bread,
    trimmed, cubed

• Preheat oven to 350° (175° C).

• Beat eggs in bowl and add milk,
  sausage and cheese. Pour over
  bread and mix well.

• Pour into sprayed 9 x 13-inch
  (23 x 33 cm) baking pan and
  cover with foil.

• Bake for 20 minutes. Remove
  foil and turn oven up to 375°
  (190° C) and bake for additional
  10 minutes. Serves 6.

Eggs in a Basket

2 (15 ounce) cans
    corned beef hash   2 (425 g)
6 eggs
¼ cup seasoned
    breadcrumbs   30 g
Butter

• Preheat oven to 325° (160° C).

• Spread hash evenly in sprayed
  7 x 11-inch (18 x 28 cm) baking
  dish. Press bottom of ½ cup
  (125 ml) measuring cup into
  hash to make 6 impressions.

• Break 1 egg into each
  impression. Sprinkle spoonful
  of breadcrumbs over each egg
  and top with dot of butter. Bake
  for 20 to 25 minutes or until
  eggs are as firm as desired.
  Serves 6.

Overnight Breakfast

This is "French toast" the easy way and it's not just for company! The kids will love it too.

7 cups small cubed French bread, bottom crust removed	1.6 L
¾ cup chopped pecans	85 g
1 (3 ounce) package cream cheese, softened	85 g
4 tablespoons sugar	60 g
1 (8 ounce) carton whipping cream	230 g
½ cup real maple syrup	125 ml
6 eggs, slightly beaten	
1 teaspoon vanilla	5 ml
½ teaspoon ground cinnamon	2 ml

- Place cubed bread in sprayed 9 x 13-inch (23 x 33 cm) baking dish and press down gently. Sprinkle with pecans. Beat cream cheese and sugar in bowl until fluffy and gradually mix in whipping cream and syrup.

- In separate bowl, whisk eggs, vanilla, cinnamon and about ½ teaspoon (2 ml) salt and fold into cream cheese-whipping cream mixture. Slowly pour this mixture evenly over bread. Cover and refrigerate overnight.

- When ready to bake, preheat oven to 350° (175° C).

- Remove from refrigerator 20 minutes before baking. Cover and bake for 30 minutes or until center sets and top is golden brown. To serve, cut into squares and serve with maple syrup. Serves 8.

Heavenly Eggs for the Saints

Butter
Bread
Mozzarella cheese slices
Eggs
Precooked bacon slices, heated

- Preheat oven to 350° (175° C).

- Butter slice of bread for each person and place buttered-side down into baking dish. Place cheese slice over bread.

- Separate 1 egg for each slice of bread. Add pinch of salt to egg whites in bowl and beat until stiff.

- Pile egg whites on cheese and make nest in top. Slip 1 egg yolk into each nest and bake for 20 minutes. Serve immediately.

- Cut cooked bacon in half and lay pieces over eggs like a cross. Serve immediately.

Orange French Toast

1 egg, beaten	
½ cup orange juice	125 ml
5 slices raisin bread	
1 cup crushed graham crackers	105 g
2 tablespoons butter	30 g

- Combine egg and orange juice in bowl.

- Dip each slice of bread in egg mixture and then in graham cracker crumbs.

- Fry in butter in skillet until brown. Serves 5.

Breakfast Cinnamon Cake

⅔ cup packed brown
    sugar   150 g
1 tablespoon grated
    orange peel   15 ml
2 (12 ounce) refrigerated
    cinnamon rolls   2 (340 g)

- Preheat oven to 375° (190° C).

- Combine brown sugar and orange peel in small bowl. Open cans of rolls (save frosting), cut each in quarters and coat each with cooking spray.

- Dip in sugar-orange mixture and arrange evenly in sprayed 10-inch (25 cm) bundt pan. Gently press down on each. Bake for 35 minutes until light brown and about double in size.

- Cool slightly in pan. Invert serving plate on top of pan, hold plate and pan together with oven mitts and invert. Remove pan. Spread frosting unevenly over top of cake and serve warm. Serves 6.

Cherry-Pecan Oatmeal

2 cups of your favorite
    oatmeal, cooked   160 g
½ cup dried cherries,
    chopped   60 g
½ cup packed brown
    sugar   110 g
¼ cup (½ stick) butter,
    softened   60 g
½ teaspoon ground
    cinnamon   2 ml
½ cup chopped pecans,
    toasted   55 g

- Cook your favorite oatmeal in saucepan.

- Combine cherries, brown sugar, butter and cinnamon in bowl. Stir into cooked oatmeal.

- Spoon into individual serving bowls and sprinkle toasted pecans over top of each serving. Serve 6.

Croissant French Toast with Strawberry Syrup

4 large day-old croissants
¾ cup half-and-half
   cream   **175 ml**
2 large eggs
1 teaspoon vanilla   **5 ml**
¼ cup (½ stick) butter   **60 ml**

- Slice croissants in half lengthwise. Whisk half-and-half cream, eggs and vanilla in shallow bowl. Heat 1 tablespoon (15 ml) butter at a time in large skillet.

- Dip croissant halves into egg mixture and coat well. Cook for about 2 minutes, 4 croissant halves at a time, turn and cook on both sides until light brown.

- Repeat procedure with remaining butter and croissant halves.

Strawberry Syrup:

1 quart fresh
   strawberries, sliced   **610 g**
¾ cup sugar   **150 g**
¼ cup orange juice   **60 ml**

- Combine all ingredients in saucepan and let stand for 30 minutes.

- Cook over medium-low heat, stirring occasionally for 5 to 8 minutes. Serve warm over croissant toast. Serves 4.

No-Mess Oven Pancakes

⅔ cup flour						80 g
⅔ cup milk						150 g
¼ cup sugar						50 g
5 large eggs, beaten
Canola oil
Maple syrup or fresh
	strawberries

• Preheat oven to 425° (220° C).

• Combine flour, milk, sugar and
eggs in bowl. Place a little oil
on large baking sheet and rub oil
to cover whole surface of pan.
Place in oven for 5 minutes
to heat.

• Pour pancake mixture onto pan
to make several pancakes. Bake
for about 18 minutes or until
puffy and golden.

• Serve with maple syrup and
fresh berries. Serves 3.

Breakfast Shake

1 banana, cut into
	1-inch slices				2.5 cm
1 mango, peeled, cubed
1½ cups pineapple juice
	or orange juice,
	chilled						360 ml
1 (8 ounce) container
	vanilla yogurt				230 g

• Process banana slices, mango,
juice and yogurt in blender until
smooth. Scrape sides of blender
and mix. Serve immediately.
Serves 2.

Super Salads

Veggies, Fruits, Pasta, Greens and Meats

Super Salads Contents

Zesty Bean Salad

1 (15 ounce) can kidney
    beans   425 g
1 (15 ounce) can pinto
    beans   425 g
1 (16 ounce) package
    frozen whole kernel
    corn, thawed, drained 455 g
1 red onion, chopped
1 bell pepper, seeded,
    chopped
1 (7 ounce) can chopped
    green chilies   200 g
2 cups cubed deli ham   280 g

- Rinse and drain kidney beans and pinto beans and place in salad bowl.

- Add corn, onion, bell pepper, green chilies and ham; mix well.

Dressing:

1 (8 ounce) bottle cheddar-
    parmesan ranch
    dressing   230 g
2 tablespoons lemon juice 30 ml

- Pour ranch dressing into small bowl and stir in lemon juice.

- Pour over salad and toss. Refrigerate for several hours before serving for flavors to blend. Serves 4.

*Keep your salads crisper longer by chilling
the salad plates or serving bowl.*

Easy Vegetable Salad

1 head cauliflower
1 head broccoli
1 (10 ounce) package
    frozen green peas,
    thawed   280 g
2 ribs celery, diagonally
    sliced
1 bunch fresh green
    onions, sliced
2 cups cubed deli ham   280 g

- Wash and drain cauliflower and broccoli and break into florets.

- Place in large bowl. Add peas, celery, green onions and ham; toss well.

Dressing:

2 cups mayonnaise   450 g
¼ cup sugar   50 g
1 tablespoon white
    vinegar   15 ml
1 cup shredded
    mozzarella cheese   115 g

- Combine all dressing ingredients in bowl and pour over vegetables and toss.

- Refrigerate for several hours before serving. Serves 8.

Lettuce or greens to make a salad are not required.
For a quick, "right-out-of-the-refrigerator" salad,
mix broccoli, cauliflower, celery, cucumbers, tomatoes,
green beans and anything else you find on the shelves
that might work. Pour in your favorite dressing and toss.

Green-Rice Salad

1 (10 ounce) package
   mixed baby salad
   greens   280 g
2 cups cooked rice,
   chilled   370 g
2 (11 ounce) cans
   mandarin oranges,
   drained, chilled   2 (310 g)
½ cup thinly sliced
   scallions, chilled   65 g

- Combine salad greens, rice,
  oranges and scallions in
  salad bowl.

Dressing:

1 (8 ounce) bottle Italian
   salad dressing   230 g
1 teaspoon ground cumin   5 ml
1 avocado, peeled, well
   mashed

- Combine salad dressing, cumin,
  avocado, and ½ teaspoon (2 ml)
  each of salt and pepper in jar
  with lid. Pour about half the
  dressing over salad and toss.
  Add more as needed. Serves 6.

Harmony Salad

2 heads red leaf
   lettuce, torn
2 (11 ounce) cans
   mandarin oranges,
   drained   2 (310 g)
2 avocados, peeled,
   cubed
1 red onion, sliced
1 (8 ounce) bottle red
   wine vinaigrette
   dressing   230 g
¼ cup sunflower
   kernels   30 g

- Place lettuce, oranges, avocados
  and onion slices in salad bowl;
  refrigerate.

- Drizzle about half salad dressing
  over salad, toss, using more if
  needed. Sprinkle sunflower
  kernels over top of salad.
  Serves 4.

Fruit and Greens Delight

2 (10 ounce) bags
  radicchio salad
  mix   2 (280 g)
2 golden delicious
  apples, cored,
  cut in wedges
1¼ cups crumbled
  blue cheese   170 g
⅔ cup chopped
  walnuts   85 g

- Combine all salad ingredients in salad bowl.

Dressing:

⅔ cup applesauce   170 g
⅓ cup olive oil   75 ml
⅓ cup cider vinegar 75 ml
1 tablespoon dijon-style
  mustard   15 ml

- Combine vinaigrette dressing ingredients in small bowl and mix well. Toss with salad. Serves 4.

TIP: If you slice the apples several minutes before serving, sprinkle 1 tablespoon (15 ml) lemon juice over them and toss so they will not turn dark.

Radicchio [rah-DEE-kee-oh] has a deep red leaf with white ribs and looks similar to red cabbage. Small amounts add a nice accent to other salad greens; arugula tastes bitter and peppery-tasting when eaten alone.

Pasta Toss

1 (8 ounce) package bow-tie pasta	230 g
1 tablespoon olive oil	15 ml
2 cups diagonally sliced carrots	245 g
2 cups broccoli florets	140 g
1 red bell pepper	
1 yellow bell pepper	
2 cups cooked, cubed ham	280 g

- Cook pasta according to package directions. Drain pasta and add olive oil and cool.

- Add carrots, broccoli, bell peppers and ham.

Dressing:

¾ cup creamy Italian salad dressing	175 ml
2 tablespoons balsamic vinegar	30 ml
1 tablespoon sugar	15 ml
½ teaspoon seasoned salt	2 ml
½ teaspoon seasoned pepper	2 ml

- Combine dressing ingredients in bowl and pour over vegetables and toss.

- Refrigerate for several hours before serving. Serves 6.

The main difference between the names of plain pasta are the shapes. While the taste is the same, certain shapes of pasta work better in certain recipes. The more complex the design, the more sauce will stick to the pasta.

Super Summer Salad Supreme

⅓ pound cooked deli
   roast beef, cubed   170 g
1 (15 ounce) can 3-bean
   salad, chilled, drained 425 g
1 (8 ounce) block
   mozzarella cheese,
   cubed   230 g
1 (10 ounce) bag mixed
   salad greens with
   Italian dressing   280 g

- Lightly toss beef, 3-bean salad and cheese in large salad bowl. Pour in just enough salad dressing to moisten greens. Serves 6 to 8.

TIP: Substitute turkey or ham for beef and Swiss cheese for mozzarella.

Pasta and Lemon Pea Salad

1 pound bow-tie pasta   455 g
1 (10 ounce) package
   frozen baby green
   peas, thawed   280 g
½ cup mayonnaise   110 g
2 tablespoons lemon juice 30 ml
½ cup whipping cream 40 g
2 cups cooked, cubed
   ham   280 g

- Cook pasta as according to package directions. Add peas last 2 minutes of cooking time. Drain pasta and peas, rinse in cold water and drain again.

- Transfer to large salad bowl. Combine mayonnaise with lemon juice, 1 teaspoon (5 ml) salt, a little pepper in bowl and stir in cream and ham.

- Fold mayonnaise mixture into pasta and peas and toss to coat well. Refrigerate for several hours before serving. Serves 6.

Gourmet Couscous Salad

1 (10 ounce) box
  chicken-flavored
  couscous   280 g
2 tomatoes, coarsely
  chopped
2 zucchini, coarsely
  chopped
4 fresh green onions,
  sliced
1 cup cubed deli turkey   140 g
1 cup crumbled feta
  cheese   135 g

- Cook couscous according to package directions, but do not use butter.

- Combine tomatoes, zucchini, green onions, turkey and couscous in salad bowl.

Dressing:

1 tablespoon lemon juice   15 ml
¼ cup olive oil   60 ml
½ teaspoon dried basil   2 ml
½ teaspoon seasoned
  black pepper   2 ml

- Combine dressing ingredients in pint jar with lid and shake until they blend well.

- When ready to serve, add feta cheese, pour dressing over salad and toss. Refrigerate. Serves 6.

Couscous is a fine, tiny, round Middle Eastern pasta that is often thought of as a grain. It can be served as a breakfast cereal, dressed as a salad, sweetened for a dessert or a side dish.

Italian Salad

1 (10 ounce) package
    mixed salad greens   280 g
1 cup shredded
    mozzarella cheese   115 g
1 (2 ounce) can sliced
    ripe black olives   60 g
1 (15 ounce) can
    cannelloni beans,
    rinsed, drained   425 g
1 (8 ounce) bottle zesty
    Italian dressing   230 g

- Combine greens, cheese, olives and cannelloni beans in salad bowl. Toss with salad dressing.

- Serve with Italian bread and cheeses, if you like. Serves 6.

Toss the Greens

1 (10 ounce) package
    mixed salad greens   280 g
1½ cups halved cherry
    tomatoes   225 g
1 cucumber, sliced
1 red onion, sliced in rings
1 pound seasoned, cooked
    chicken breasts, cut
    into strips   455 g

Dressing:

Italian salad dressing
Lots of seasoned black
    pepper
¼ teaspoon cayenne
    pepper   1 ml

- Combine greens, tomatoes, cucumber and onion rings in large salad bowl and toss. When ready to serve, toss with salad dressing.

- Arrange salad on individual salad plates, top with strips of chicken and sprinkle with seasoned black pepper and cayenne pepper. Serves 6 to 8.

Rainbow Pasta Salad

1 (16 ounce) package
   tri-color spiral pasta   455 g
1 red bell pepper, thinly
   sliced
1 yellow bell pepper,
   thinly sliced
4 small zucchini, with
   peel, sliced
3 ribs celery, sliced
   diagonally
1 cup cooked, chopped
   ham   140 g
Lettuce
Breadsticks

- Cook pasta according to package direction; rinse in cold water and drain well. Combine pasta, bell peppers, zucchini, celery and ham in large bowl.

Dressing:

1 (14 ounce) can
   sweetened condensed
   milk   400 g
1 cup white vinegar   200 g
1¼ cups mayonnaise   280 g
2 teaspoons seasoned
   pepper   10 ml

- Combine sweetened condensed milk, vinegar, mayonnaise and seasoned pepper in small bowl.

- Pour half dressing over salad, using more if needed. Toss well, cover and refrigerate overnight.

- Serve over bed of lettuce with breadsticks. Serves 6 to 8.

When you wash lettuce and greens for a salad, be sure to dry the leaves between paper towels. Dressing will be watered down if water is left on the leaves.

Chunky Egg Salad

12 eggs, hard-boiled,
    quartered
⅓ cup sun-dried tomato
    GourMayo®   75 g
2 ribs celery, sliced
½ cup sliced, stuffed
    green olives   65 g
Lettuce leaves
Crackers

• Place all ingredients in salad
  bowl and add a little salt and
  pepper.

• Gently toss and serve over bed
  of lettuce leaves with crackers.
  Serves 4.

*TIP: This is also great stuffed
    in hollowed-out tomato,
    bell pepper or melon. And
    if you are really in a hurry,
    just put it between 2 slices
    of dark bread.*

Spinach Salad

1 (10 ounce) bag baby
    spinach   280 g
1 cup fresh sliced
    strawberries   165 g
1 (3 ounce) package
    slivered almonds,
    toasted   85 g
½ cup crumbled feta
    cheese   70 g
1 cup cooked, shredded
    turkey breast   140 g

• Combine all ingredients in salad
  bowl and toss with dressing.

Dressing:

½ cup sugar   100 g
¼ cup white wine vinegar 60 ml
⅓ cup olive oil   75 ml
2 teaspoons poppy seeds   10 ml

• Combine all ingredients in bowl
  and toss with spinach mixture.
  Serves 6.

Super Summer Salad

1 (10 ounce) box orzo
    pasta   280 g
1 (10 ounce) package
    frozen broccoli florets,
    thawed   280 g
1 (10 ounce) package
    frozen green beans,
    thawed   280 g
1 (12 ounce) jar baby
    corn nuggets, drained   340 g
2 cups cooked, cubed ham 280 g

- Cook orzo in large saucepan according to package directions. Stir in broccoli and green beans for 5 minutes before orzo is done.

- Boil and cook for an additional 5 minutes. Drain well. Transfer pasta and vegetables to salad bowl and add corn and ham.

Dressing:

1 teaspoon seasoned salt   5 ml
1 (8 ounce) jar sweet-
    and-sour sauce   170 g
2 tablespoons olive oil   30 ml

- Sprinkle with seasoned salt, pour on sweet-and-sour sauce and olive oil and toss. Serves 8.

The name of the small rice-shaped pasta known as "orzo" means "barley".

Chicken Caesar Salad

4 boneless, skinless chicken
   breast halves, grilled
1 (10 ounce) package
   romaine salad greens   280 g
½ cup grated parmesan
   cheese   50 g
1 cup seasoned croutons   40 g
¾ cup Caesar or Italian
   dressing   175 ml

- Cut chicken breasts into
  strips. Combine chicken,
  salad greens, cheese and
  croutons in large bowl.

- When ready to serve, toss with
  salad dressing. Serves 8.

Colorful Salad Toss

2 (8 ounce) packages
   baby spinach,
   stems removed   2 (230 g)
1 small head
   cauliflower, cut
   into small florets
1 red bell pepper,
   seeded, cut in strips
¾ cup whole walnuts   90 g
½ cup toasted
   sunflower seeds   65 g
2 cups cooked,
   chopped ham   280 g
Berry vinaigrette

- Combine spinach, cauliflower,
  bell pepper strips, walnuts,
  sunflower seeds and ham and a
  generous amount of salt in large
  salad bowl.

- Toss with strawberry or
  raspberry vinaigrette salad
  dressing. Serves 8.

Friday-After-Thanksgiving Salad

2 (10 ounce) packages
   romaine lettuce   2 (280 g)
2½ - 3 cups cooked,
   sliced turkey   350 - 420 g
1 (8 ounce) jar baby
   corn, quartered   230 g
2 tomatoes, chopped
1 (8 ounce) package
   shredded colby
   cheese   230 g

- Combine romaine lettuce, turkey, baby corn, tomatoes and cheese in large salad bowl.

Dressing:

⅔ cup mayonnaise	150 g
⅔ cup salsa	175 g
¼ cup cider vinegar	60 ml
2 tablespoons sugar	30 ml

- Combine all dressing ingredients in bowl and mix well.

- When ready to serve, sprinkle on a little salt and pepper, pour dressing over salad and toss to coat well. Serves 8.

TIP: If you want to make this leftover dish an even "bigger and better" salad, just add some ripe olives, red onion, black beans or the precooked bacon.

Fiesta Holiday Salad

This is great for that leftover holiday turkey!

1 (10 ounce) package torn
   romaine lettuce   **280 g**
3 cups cooked, diced
   smoked turkey   **420 g**
1 (15 ounce) can black
   beans, rinsed, drained **425 g**
2 tomatoes, quartered,
   drained

- Combine lettuce, turkey, beans and tomatoes in large salad bowl.

Dressing:

⅔ cup mayonnaise   **150 g**
¾ cup prepared salsa   **200 g**

- Combine mayonnaise and salsa.

- When ready to serve, spoon dressing over salad and toss. If you like, a sliced red onion can be added to salad. Serves 8.

TIP: For a little extra touch, you might sprinkle crumbed bacon over top of salad. You can buy the real, cooked, crumbled bacon in the grocery store if you don't have time to fry some.

Washing and storing lettuce properly will make a big difference in how long it will stay salad-fresh. Remove any bruised, wilted or brown-edged pieces. Separate leaves and wash under cold running water. Use a salad spinner to dry the lettuce and break large pieces to fit in the spinner. Layer dry leaves between paper towels and store in a resealable plastic bag. It should keep 5 to 7 days. When ready to serve green salad, tear your fresh lettuce and toss with ingredients at the last minute.

Beefy Green Salad

⅓ pound deli roast beef   140 g
1 (15 ounce) can 3-bean
    salad, chilled, drained   425 g
½ pound mozzarella
    cheese, cubed   230 g
1 (8 ounce) bag mixed
    salad greens with
    Italian dressing   230 g
Salad dressing

- Cut beef in thin strips. Lightly toss beef, 3-bean salad and cheese in large salad bowl. Pour in just enough salad dressing to moisten greens. Serves 8.

TIP: Substitute turkey or ham for beef and Swiss cheese for mozzarella.

Black Bean Chicken Salad

3 - 4 boneless, skinless
    chicken breast halves,
    cooked, cubed
1 (15 ounce) can black
    beans, drained   425 g
1 bunch green onions,
    chopped
1 cup chopped celery   100 g

- Combine chicken, black beans, onions and celery in bowl.

Dressing:

¾ cup virgin olive oil   175 ml
¼ cup lemon juice   60 ml
2 teaspoons dijon-style
    mustard   10 ml
2 teaspoons ground cumin 10 ml

- Combine all dressing ingredients in bowl and mix well.

- Pour dressing over black bean-chicken salad, toss and refrigerate. Serves 6.

Supper Ready Beef and Bean Salad

¾ pound deli roast
    beef, cut in strips   340 g
2 (15 ounce) cans
    kidney beans,
    rinsed, drained   2 (425 g)
1 cup chopped onion   160 g
1 cup chopped celery   100 g
3 eggs, hard-boiled,
    chopped
Lettuce

- Combine beef strips, beans, onion, celery and eggs in salad bowl.

Dressing:

⅓ cup mayonnaise   75 g
⅓ cup chipotle-chili
    GourMayo®   75 g
¼ cup ketchup   70 g
¼ cup sweet pickle relish   60 g
2 tablespoons olive oil   30 ml

- Combine mayonnaise, chipotle-chili GourMayo®, ketchup, pickle relish in bowl and oil and mix well.

- Spoon over beef-bean mixture and toss. Refrigerate several hours before serving.

- Rather than serving in salad bowl, shred lettuce on serving plate and serve beef-bean salad over lettuce. Serves 8.

Fruited Pork Salad Lunch

Salad:

1 (10 ounce) package fresh green salad mix	280 g
2 cups halved, seedless green grapes	300 g
1 cup fresh strawberries	165 g
1 cup refrigerated red grapefruit sections with juice	155 g
½ - ¾ pound pork tenderloin, cooked, thinly sliced, chilled	230 - 340 g

- Toss salad mix, green grapes, strawberries and grapefruit sections in salad bowl. Arrange salad on individual plates and place tenderloin slices over top.

Dressing:

¼ cup juice from grapefruit sections	60 ml
2 tablespoons red wine vinegar	30 ml
2 tablespoons oil	30 ml
1 teaspoon poppy seeds	5 ml
2 teaspoons honey	10 ml

- Mix all dressing ingredients in bowl and pour dressing over top of salads. Serves 8.

Grilled Chicken with Broccoli Slaw

Chicken:

1 (3½ pound) chicken, quartered	1.4 kg
3 tablespoons olive oil	45 ml
⅔ cup bottled barbecue sauce	150 ml

- Brush chicken quarters with olive oil and sprinkle with a little salt and pepper.

- Grill for 30 to 35 minutes and turn once or twice until juices run clear when thigh part is pierced and meat thermometer registers 170° (75° C) when inserted into chicken.

- Brush with barbecue sauce and grill just until sauce browns, but do not char.

Slaw:

¼ cup mayonnaise	55 g
3 tablespoons cider vinegar	45 ml
2 tablespoons sugar	30 ml
1 (12 ounce) package broccoli slaw	340 g

- Combine mayonnaise, vinegar and sugar in bowl and mix well.

- Spoon over broccoli slaw and toss. Refrigerate until ready to serve. Serves 6.

About 80% of the sodium in our diets are in commercial, processed foods. By preparing our own foods, we can control the amount of sodium in what we eat.

Strawberry-Chicken Salad

1 pound boneless, skinless
    chicken breast halves   455 g
Olive oil
1 (10 ounce) package
    spring greens mix   280 g
1 pint fresh strawberries,
    sliced   455 g
½ cup chopped walnuts   45 g

Dressing:

¾ cup honey   255 g
⅔ cup red wine vinegar   150 ml
1 tablespoon soy sauce   15 ml
½ teaspoon ground ginger 2 ml

- Cut chicken into strips and place in large skillet with a little oil. Cook on medium-high heat for about 10 minutes and stir occasionally.

- While chicken cooks, combine all dressing ingredients in bowl and mix well.

- After chicken strips cook for 10 minutes, pour ½ cup (125 ml) dressing into skillet with chicken and cook for an additional 2 minutes or until liquid evaporates.

- In separate bowl, combine spring greens mix, strawberries and walnuts, pour on remaining dressing and toss. Top with chicken strips. Serves 6.

Hawaiian Chicken Salad

3 cups cooked, diced chicken breasts	420 g
1 (20 ounce) can pineapple tidbits, well-drained	570 g
1 cup halved red grapes	150 g
1 cup chopped celery	100 g
1 large banana	

- Combine chicken, pineapple, grapes and celery in bowl and toss. Cover and refrigerate.

Dressing:

¾ cup mayonnaise	180 ml
½ cup poppy seed dressing	120 ml
½ cup salted peanuts	120 ml

- Combine mayonnaise, poppy seed dressing and a sprinkle of salt in bowl.

- When ready to serve, slice bananas and add to salad.

- Top with mayonnaise-poppy seed dressing and toss. Just before serving, sprinkle peanuts over top of salad. Serves 8.

Peanuts contain healthy monounsaturated fats as well as vitamin E, folic acid, magnesium, copper, fiber and plant proteins. They are naturally cholesterol-free, help to control cholesterol levels and have almost none of the bad trans fats.

Barbecue Chicken Salad

Here's a quickie with that "it-takes-a-long-time" flavor.

Dressing:

¾ cup ranch dressing   175 ml
3 tablespoons barbecue
    sauce   45 ml
2 tablespoons salsa   30 ml

- Combine all dressing ingredients in bowl. Refrigerate and set aside.

Salad:

3 boneless, skinless chicken
    breast halves, grilled
1 (9 ounce) package
    romaine lettuce   255 ml
1 (15 ounce) can seasoned
    black beans,
    rinsed, drained   425 g
12 - 15 cherry tomatoes

- Cut chicken breasts in strips and heat in oven just enough to warm thoroughly.

- Place chicken strips, cut-up romaine, black beans and cherry tomatoes in bowl.

- Toss enough dressing with salad to lightly coat. Serves 8.

TIP: The next time you grill, just grill some extra chicken breasts and freeze them to use for this dish. Or if you don't have time to grill chicken, just use deli smoked turkey.

Apple-Walnut Chicken Salad

3 - 4 boneless, skinless
   chicken breast halves,
   cooked, cubed
2 tart green apples,
   peeled, chopped
½ cup chopped pitted
   dates   75 g
1 cup finely chopped
   celery   100 g

- Combine chicken, apples, dates and celery in bowl.

Dressing:

½ cup chopped walnuts	45 g
⅓ cup sour cream	80 g
⅓ cup mayonnaise	80 g
1 tablespoon lemon juice	15 ml

- Preheat oven to 300° (150° C).

- Toast walnuts for 10 minutes.

- Combine sour cream, mayonnaise and lemon juice in bowl and mix well. Add walnuts.

- Pour dressing over chicken salad and toss. Refrigerate. Serves 8.

How many times during our childhoods did we hear the adage, "An apple a day keeps the doctor away." As it turns out, the truth is the apple is a very nutritious food. Apples contain vitamin C plus many other antioxidants, which are cancer fighters.

Tarragon-Chicken Salad

1 cup chopped pecans	110 g
3 - 4 boneless, skinless chicken breast halves, cooked, cubed	
1 cup chopped celery	100 g
¾ cup peeled, chopped cucumbers	90 g

- Preheat oven to 300° (150° C).

- Place pecans in shallow pan and toast for 10 minutes.

- Combine chicken, celery and cucumbers in bowl.

Dressing:

⅔ cup mayonnaise	150 g
1 tablespoon lemon juice	15 ml
2 tablespoons tarragon vinegar	30 ml
1¼ teaspoons crumbled, dried tarragon	6 ml

- Combine all dressing ingredients in bowl and mix well.

- When ready to serve, toss with chicken mixture and add pecans. Serves 8.

Chop – cut into small, irregular pieces about ¼ inch in size.

Southwestern Chicken Salad

4 cups cubed, cooked
   chicken breasts   560 g
1 (15 ounce) can black
   beans, drained   425 g
¾ red onion, chopped
½ red bell pepper,
   chopped
½ yellow bell pepper,
   chopped
¼ cup chopped fresh
   cilantro   5 g
½ cup sour cream   120 g
¼ cup mayonnaise   55 g
½ teaspoon garlic powder 2 ml
1 jalapeno pepper, seeded,
   finely chopped
1 teaspoon lime juice   5 ml
½ cup pine nuts, toasted   65 g
Lettuce

- Combine chicken, beans, onion, bell peppers and cilantro in large bowl.

- In separate bowl, whisk sour cream and mayonnaise.

- Stir in garlic powder, jalapeno pepper and lime juice and add to chicken. Add a little salt and pepper and toss.

- Refrigerate for at least 1 hour. Just before serving, toss in pine nuts. Serve on bed of lettuce. Serves 8.

To quickly chop an onion, slice off the stem and root ends and remove peel. Halve the onion from top to root end. Place each onion half flat side down and make ¼-inch vertical slices. Holding the vertical slices together, cut ¼-inch horizontal slices. There you go!

Mexican Chicken Salad

3 - 4 boneless, skinless
  chicken breast halves,
  cooked, cubed
1 (15 ounce) can green
  peas, drained   425 g
1 red bell pepper, seeded,
  diced
1 green bell pepper,
  seeded, diced
1 cup chopped celery   100 g

- Combine all ingredients in bowl and serve with dressing.

Dressing:

1½ cups sour cream   360 g
2 tablespoons chili sauce 35 g
2 teaspoons ground cumin 10 ml
1 small bunch cilantro,
  minced

- Combine all dressing ingredients in bowl and add a little salt and pepper.

- Pour over chicken salad and toss. Refrigerate before serving. Serves 8.

Spinach-Turkey Salad Supper

2 (8 ounce) packages
  baby spinach   2 (230 g)
⅓ cup whole walnuts 40 g
⅓ cup Craisins®   40 g
2 red delicious apples
  with peel, sliced
¾ pound deli smoked
  turkey, cubed   340 g
½ cup honey-mustard
  salad dressing   125 ml

- Combine spinach, walnuts, Craisins®, apples and turkey in large salad bowl

- Toss with salad dressing.

Noodle-Turkey Salad

1 (3 ounce) package
  oriental-flavor ramen
  noodle soup mix   85 g
1 (16 ounce) package
  finely shredded
  coleslaw mix   455 g
¾ pound deli smoked
  turkey, cut into strips 340 g
½ cup vinaigrette salad
  dressing   125 ml

- Coarsely crush noodles and
  place in bowl with lid. Add
  coleslaw mix and turkey strips.

- Combine vinaigrette salad
  dressing and seasoning packet
  from noodle mix in small bowl.

- Pour over noodle-turkey mixture
  and toss to coat mixture well.
  Refrigerate. Serves 8.

Chicken-Grapefruit Salad Supper

1 (10 ounce) package
  romaine salad mix   280 g
1 (24 ounce) jar
  grapefruit sections,
  drained   680 g
1 rotisserie-cooked
  chicken, boned, cubed
½ red onion, sliced

- Combine salad mix, grapefruit
  sections, chicken and onion in
  salad bowl

Dressing:

2 tablespoons orange juice 30 ml
2 tablespoons white wine
  vinegar   30 ml
2 tablespoons extra-
  virgin olive oil   30 ml

- Combine all dressing ingredients
  plus 1 teaspoon (5 ml) each of
  salt and pepper in small bowl.
  Pour over salad and toss.
  Serves 8.

Bridge Club Luncheon Favorite

1 rotisserie-cooked
   chicken
1 cup red grapes, halved   150 g
1 cup green grapes,
   halved   150 g
2 cups chopped celery   200 g
⅔ cup whole walnuts   80 g
⅔ cup sliced fresh onion   110 g

• Skin chicken and cut chicken breast in thin strips. (Save dark meat for another meal or use frozen, grilled chicken breasts.) Place in bowl with lid.

• Add red and green grapes, celery, walnuts and sliced onions.

Dressing:

½ cup mayonnaise   110 g
1 tablespoon orange juice   15 ml
2 tablespoons red wine
   vinegar   30 ml
1 teaspoon chili powder   5 ml

• Combine all dressing ingredients in bowl, add a little salt and pepper and mix well. Spoon over salad mixture and toss. Refrigerate. Serves 6 to 8.

Wine vinegars are made from red or white wine and derive flavor from the type of wine used.

Herbed Chicken Salad

1 rotisserie-cooked chicken
¼ cup chopped fresh
   chives   5 g
2 tablespoons capers   30 ml
1 cup chopped celery   100 g
1 cup chopped sweet
   pickles   245 g

- Skin chicken and cut meat from bones. Slice chicken in thin strips and place in bowl.

- Add chives, capers, celery and sweet pickles and mix well.

Dressing:

¼ cup extra-virgin
   olive oil   60 ml
3 tablespoons white wine
   vinegar   45 ml
1 teaspoon chopped fresh
   thyme   5 ml
1 teaspoon oregano   5 ml
1 tablespoon honey   15 ml

- Whisk olive oil, vinegar, thyme, oregano, honey and a little salt and pepper in bowl. Spoon over chicken salad and toss. Refrigerate. Serves 8.

Fresh chives are in the same family as onions, scallions and garlic. They are high in vitamin C, folic acid and potassium. They have high concentrations of sulfur compounds and essential oils capable of healing properties. Beside the distinctive flavor of chives, they may help the body fight bacteria, ease stomach distress and aid in heart attack and stroke prevention by helping the body digest fat.

Old-Fashioned Chicken or Turkey Salad

3 cups cooked, cubed chicken or turkey	420 g
⅔ cup chopped celery	70 g
¾ cup sweet pickle relish	185 g
1 bunch fresh green onions with tops, chopped	
3 eggs, hard-boiled, chopped	
¾ cup mayonnaise	170 g
Lettuce leaves	

- Combine chicken, celery, relish, onions and eggs in bowl.

- Toss with mayonnaise and refrigerate. Serve on lettuce leaves. Serves 6.

Fancy Chicken or Turkey Salad

3 cups cooked, cubed chicken or turkey	420 g
1 cup chopped celery	100 g
1½ cups halved green grapes	225 g
¾ cup cashew nuts	105 g
¾ cup mayonnaise	170 g
1 cup chow mein noodles	55 g
Cabbage leaves	

- Combine chicken, celery, grapes and cashews in bowl; toss with mayonnaise.

- Just before serving, mix in noodles and serve on cabbage leaves. Serves 6.

Chicken and Rice Salad

3 cups cooked, cubed chicken or turkey	420 g
1 (6 ounce) box long grain-wild rice, cooked, drained	170 g
1 bunch fresh green onions with tops, chopped	
1 cup chopped walnuts	85 g
1 (8 ounce) can sliced water chestnuts	230 g
1 cup mayonnaise	225 g
¾ teaspoon curry powder	4 ml
Lettuce	

- Combine chicken, rice, onions, walnuts and water chestnuts in bowl. Toss with mayonnaise and curry powder and refrigerate. Serve on bed of lettuce. Serves 8.

Supper-Ready Shrimp Salad

1 (14 ounce) package frozen tortellini, cooked	400 g
1 pound cooked, peeled, veined shrimp	455 g
½ cup sliced ripe olives	65 g
½ cup chopped celery	50 g
½ cup zesty Italian salad dressing	125 ml

- Combine tortellini, shrimp, olives and celery in salad bowl.

- Pour salad dressing over salad and toss. Serve immediately or refrigerate until ready to serve. Serves 8.

Wacky Tuna Salad

1 (7 ounce) package
   cooked, light tuna
   in water   200 g
1 red apple with peel,
   cored, chopped
1 (10 ounce) package
   frozen green peas,
   thawed, drained   280 g
1 red bell pepper, chopped
Shredded lettuce

- Place tuna in bowl, add chopped apple, green peas and bell pepper and mix well.

Dressing:

½ (8 ounce) bottle
   sweet honey Catalina
   salad dressing   ½ (250 ml)
½ cup mayonnaise   112 g

- Combine dressing and mayonnaise in bowl, pour over tuna salad and stir to blend well.

- Refrigerate for at least 2 hours and serve over bed of shredded lettuce. Serves 6.

Thaw frozen foods in refrigerator or in the microwave, never at room temperature which allows unsafe bacterial growth.

Tuna-Tortellini Salad

1 (7 ounce) package tortellini	200 g
¼ cup (½ stick) butter	115 g
1 (12 ounce) can tuna, drained	340 g
1 (4 ounce) can sliced ripe olives	115 g

- Cook spaghetti according to package directions and drain. Add butter and stir until butter melts. Add tuna and olives.

Dressing:

¾ cup whipping cream	55 g
1 teaspoon dried basil leaves	5 ml
2 tablespoons parmesan cheese	15 g
1 teaspoon seasoned salt	5 ml

- Combine whipping cream, basil, cheese and seasoned salt in bowl. Pour over spaghetti-tuna mixture and toss. Serves 6.

Ribbon or strand pastas are long, flat noodles of varying length, width and thickness.

Capelli d'angelo	*"angel hair" pasta; very thin spaghetti*
Fedellini	*very thin spaghetti*
Fettucini	*"little ribbons"; long flat egg noodles*
Lasagna	*long noodles usually with rippled edges*
Linguine	*long, narrow noodles about ⅛ inch wide*
Margherite	*long, narrow noodles with one rippled edge*
Pappardelle	*long, flat noodles about with rippled edges*
Spaghetti	*long, thin strands*
Tagliatelle	*long, flat egg noodles about ¼ inch wide*
Vermicelli	*very thin spaghetti similar to angel hair pasta*

Sassy Sandwiches

Hot, Cold, Open-Face, Veggies and Meats

Sassy Sandwiches Contents

Hot Roast Beef Sandwich

1 (12 ounce) loaf
    French bread   340 g
¼ cup creamy dijon-style
    mustard   60 g
¾ pound sliced deli
    roast beef   340 g
8 slices American cheese

- Preheat oven to 325° (160° C).

- Split French bread and spread mustard on bottom slice. Line slices of beef over mustard and cheese slices over beef. Add top loaf.

- Cut loaf in quarters and place on baking sheet. Heat for about 5 minutes or until cheese just partially melts. Serves 4.

Reuben Sandwiches

12 slices dark rye bread
6 slices Swiss cheese
12 thin deli slices
    corned beef
4 cups deli coleslaw,
    drained   500 g

- On 6 slices of rye bread, layer cheese, 2 slices corned beef and lots of coleslaw. Top with remaining bread slices. Serves 6.

A Different Sandwich

Dressing:

½ cup mayonnaise   110 g
⅓ cup dijon-style
    mustard   85 g
¼ cup horseradish   55 g

Bread:

6 (7 inch) Italian
    focaccia
    flatbreads   6 (18 cm)

Filling:

1 pound deli-shaved
    roast beef   455 g
1 (12 ounce) jar roasted
    red bell peppers, cut
    in strips   340 g
6 slices mozzarella cheese
Baby romaine lettuce

- Combine dressing ingredients in small bowl. Use serrated knife to slice bread shells in half horizontally.

- Spread generous amount dressing on one side of bread.

- Top with several slices roast beef, roasted peppers, cheese, romaine and remaining bread half.

- To serve, cut sandwiches in half. Serves 6.

Tasty Sub Sandwich

4 (6 inch) sub rolls   **4 (15 cm)**

Filling:

**1 onion, halved, thinly
    sliced**
Olive oil
2 tablespoons butter   30 ml
**2 tablespoons beef
    bouillon
    granules   30 ml**
8 sliced deli roast beef
4 slices provolone cheese

- Slice rolls in half lengthwise, place on baking sheet and broil until golden brown.

- Preheat oven to 350° (175° C).

- Cook onion with a little oil in skillet on medium-low heat for 6 minutes. Set aside.

- Heat butter, ½ cup (125 ml) water and beef granules in saucepan. Use tongs to dip beef slices into hot liquid.

- Place beef slices and cheese slices on bottom of 4 rolls. Divide cooked onion over cheese and place top rolls over onions.

- Place filled sub rolls on baking sheet and heat for 5 minutes or just until cheese melts. Serves 4.

It is a fact that most people have the same dozen or so meals for breakfast, lunch and dinner. They usually rotate these and introduce some minor variations throughout most of their lives. Choose your meals wisely.

Southwest Burgers

8 kaiser buns
**2 pounds lean ground
  beef   910 g**
**1 (1 ounce) packet taco
  seasoning mix   30 g**
1 cup salsa, divided   265 g
**8 slices hot pepper
  Jack cheese**

- Combine beef, taco seasoning and ¼ cup (65 g) salsa in large bowl. Shape mixture into 8 patties.

- If you are grilling, cook patties for about 12 minutes or until they cook thoroughly and turn once.

- To broil in oven, place patties on broiler pan 4 to 5 inches (10 to 13 cm) from heat and broil until they cook thoroughly. Turn once during cooking.

- When patties are almost done, place buns cut-side down on grill and heat for 1 or 2 minutes.

- Place 8 patties on bottom half of buns, top with cheese and cook for an additional 1 minute or until cheese melts.

- Top with heaping tablespoon of salsa and top half of bun. Serves 8.

*Limp vegetables like celery, carrots and even potatoes
will regain their crispness and crunch when you
soak them in ice water for about 1 hour.*

It's a Tortilla Wrap

3 large (12 inch) garden
   spinach tortillas   3 (32 cm)
Mayonnaise

- Heat broiler, place tortillas on baking sheet and broil briefly on each side.

- Remove from oven and spread thin layer of mayonnaise over 1 side of tortillas.

Filling:

1 cup shredded cheddar cheese	115 g
1 (9 ounce) package spring salad mix	255 g
1 cup finely diced, drained tomatoes	180 g
3 finely chopped green onions	
6 slices thin deli turkey or ham	

- Sprinkle cheese over tortillas and return to oven just until cheese melts.

- Combine salad mix, tomatoes and green onions in bowl and sprinkle on tortillas. Place 2 slices of turkey or ham on tortillas. Roll or fold over. Serves 3.

Sprouted grain breads are easier to digest, are more nutritious and maintain freshness longer than other breads. They can be found in the freezer or refrigerator section in the grocery store.

A Family Sandwich

1 (8 ounce) loaf French bread	230 g
1 (11 ounce) bottle creamy dijon GourMayo®	310 g
6 ounces sliced Swiss cheese	170 g
6 ounces sliced deli ham	170 g
8 sandwich-sliced dill pickles	

- Preheat oven to 375° (190° C).

- Cut bread in half horizontally and spread dijon-GourMayo® over cut sides of bread.

- Arrange half of cheese and half of ham on bottom slice and top with pickle slices. Spread remaining cheese and ham on top of pickles.

- Cover with top of bread, press down on sandwich and cut into quarters. Place on baking sheet and bake for 5 minutes. Serve hot. Serve 4.

Open-Face Apple-Ham Sandwiches

Mayonnaise
Mustard
4 kaiser rolls
16 slices American cheese
8 thin slices deli, boiled ham
1 red delicious apple with peel, finely chopped

- Spread a little mayonnaise and mustard on top and bottom of 4 kaiser rolls and place on baking sheet.

- Top each bottom and top with 1 slice of cheese, slice ham and about 2 tablespoons (15 g) chopped apple. Top with remaining cheese slices.

- Broil 4 to 5 inches (10 to 13 cm) from heat just until top slice of cheese melts. Serve immediately. Serves 8.

Wrap It Up Now!

4 burrito-size flour tortillas
¼ cup sweet-honey
    Catalina dressing   60 ml
4 slices deli ham
4 slices Swiss cheese
1½ cups deli coleslaw   190 g

- Spread tortillas with dressing and add 1 slice ham and 1 slice cheese on each tortilla. Spoon one-fourth of coleslaw on top.

- Roll and wrap each in wax paper. Place in microwave and heat just until cheese melts. Cut wraps in half to serve. Serves 4.

Chicken Sandwich Olé

1 (10 ounce) package
    frozen breaded
    chicken breast patties 280 g
Hoagie buns
½ cup prepared black
    bean dip   110 g
⅓ cup thick-and-chunky
    hot salsa   90 g
Lettuce, shredded
Tomatoes, chopped

- Preheat oven to 325° (160° C).

- Heat chicken breast patties in oven according to package directions

- Place 4 split hoagie buns in oven the last 3 minutes of cooking time.

- Spread bottom half of each hoagie liberally with bean dip and salsa. Top each with chicken patty, shredded lettuce and chopped tomatoes.

- Place top bun over lettuce and tomatoes. Serve immediately. Serves 4.

A Special Grilled Cheese Sandwich

Make as many of these sandwiches ad you need. Just multiply the ingredients below by the number you need.

Butter, softened
1 loaf 7-grain bread
Filling for 1 sandwich:
2 tablespoons chipotle
    GourMayo®   **30 g**
2 slices sharp cheddar
    cheese
2 tablespoons real
    crumbled bacon   **10 g**
¼ whole avocado,
    thinly sliced

- For each sandwich, spread softened butter on 2 thick slices of 7-grain bread. Place 1 slice, butter-side down in heavy skillet.

- Spread with 1 tablespoon (15 ml) GourMayo® and 1 slice cheese.

- Sprinkle with crumbled bacon and avocado slices. Top with second slice of cheese and remaining slice of bread spread with 1 tablespoon (15 ml) GourMayo®.

- Heat skillet on medium-high and cook for about 2 minutes or until light brown and cheese melts.

- Turn sandwich over and cook for an additional 2 minutes or until cheese melts completely. Serves 2.

Sunday Night Chicken Sandwiches

1 (10 ounce) package frozen breaded chicken breast patties	280 g
Olive oil	
½ (12 ounce) carton guacamole dip	½ (340 g)
⅓ cup thick-and-chunky salsa	90 g
½ (9 ounce) package shredded lettuce	½ (255 g)
4 whole wheat hamburger buns, split	

- Cook breaded chicken breast patties according to package directions in skillet with very little oil.

- Spread thin layer of guacamole dip on bottom of each bun, top each with chicken patty and spread salsa on top of patty.

- Place 3 to 4 tablespoons (15 to 20 g) shredded lettuce over salsa. Spread another thin layer of guacamole on top bun and place over each filled bottom bun. Serves 4.

Olive oil originated in Asia, but has been cultivated in the Mediterranean for thousands of years. One tablespoon of olive oil has 130 calories and 14 grams of fat, mostly monounsaturated fat that has a positive effect on cholesterol levels. It is also used for dry skin, prevention for hair loss and earaches.

Italian-Sausage Sandwiches

1 pound sweet Italian
   sausage   455 g
1 red bell pepper,
   chopped
1 onion, chopped
1⅔ cups Italian-style
   spaghetti sauce   410 g
Hoagie rolls

- Remove casing from sausage and cook sausage, bell pepper and onion in skillet over medium heat or until sausage browns.

- Stir in spaghetti sauce and heat until boiling. Simmer for 5 minutes and stir constantly. Pour mixture over split hoagie rolls. Serves 4 to 6.

Confetti Sandwiches

1 tablespoon lemon juice 15 ml
1 (8 ounce) package
   cream cheese,
   softened   225 g
½ cup grated carrots   55 g
¼ cup grated cucumber 30 g
¼ cup grated purple
   onion   40 g
¼ cup grated bell pepper 35 g

- Combine lemon juice with cream cheese and add enough mayonnaise to make cheese into a spreading consistency.

- Fold in grated vegetables, spread on bread for sandwiches and refrigerate. Serves 4.

"Honey Do" Open-Face Sandwich

⅓ cup honey-mustard
    dressing   75 ml
4 kaiser rolls, split
8 thin slices deli honey ham
8 slices Swiss cheese

- Preheat oven to 400° (205° C).

- Spread honey-mustard on each split roll. Top each with ham and cheese slices.

- Place on baking sheet and bake for 4 to 5 minutes or until cheese melts. Serves 4.

Pizza Sandwich

6 English muffins
1 pound bulk sausage,
    cooked, drained   455 g
1½ cups pizza sauce   360 ml
1 (4 ounce) can
    mushrooms, drained   115 g
1 (8 ounce) package
    shredded mozzarella
    cheese   230 g

- Split muffins and layer ingredients on each muffin half ending with cheese.

- Broil until cheese melts. Serves 6.

You can buy sausage in several forms: fresh or cured, cooked or uncooked, or dried. Read the labels carefully for cooking instructions.

Meatball Heroes

1 (16 ounce) container
   marinara sauce   **455 g**
1 (16 ounce) package
   frozen bell peppers,
   thawed   **455 g**
½ onion, minced
1 (12 ounce) package
   frozen Italian
   meatballs, thawed   **340 g**
French rolls*

- Combine marinara sauce, bell peppers and onion in large saucepan and cook on medium heat for 5 minutes.

- Add meatballs, cover and gently boil for about 5 minutes or until meatballs are hot.

- Spoon into split French rolls and serve hot. Serves 8.

*TIP: *Any bread like club rolls, hot dog buns or French rolls will work.*

Provolone-Pepper Burgers

⅓ cup finely cubed
   provolone cheese   **45 g**
¼ cup diced roasted red
   peppers   **50 g**
¼ cup finely chopped
   onion   **40 g**
1 pound lean ground beef **455 g**
4 hamburger buns, split

- Combine cheese, red peppers, onion and a little salt and pepper in bowl. Add beef, mix well and shape into 4 patties.

- Grill patties, over medium-hot heat for 5 minutes on each side or until meat is no longer pink.

- Add your favorite lettuce, tomatoes, etc., and serve on hamburger buns. Serves 4.

Turkey Asparagus Sandwiches

4 (1 ounce) slices
   cheddar cheese   4 (30 g)
2 English muffins,
   split, toasted
½ pound thinly sliced
   turkey   230 g
1 (15 ounce) can
   asparagus spears,
   drained   425 g
1 (1 ounce) package
   hollandaise sauce
   blend   30 g

- Place 1 cheese slice on each muffin half and top evenly with turkey.

- Cut asparagus spears to fit muffin halves and top each with 3 or 4 asparagus spears. (Reserve remaining asparagus for another use.)

- Prepare hollandaise sauce mix according to package directions, pour evenly over sandwiches and sprinkle with paprika, if desired. Serves 4.

Fruited Chicken Salad

1 (10 ounce) package
   spring salad mix   280 g
1 (6 ounce) package
   frozen, ready-to-serve
   chicken strips, thawed 170 g
½ cup fresh strawberries 90 g
½ cup fresh raspberries 60 g
½ fresh peach, sliced
1 (8 ounce) bottle
   raspberry salad
   dressing   230 g
Lettuce
Crackers or breadsticks

- Combine salad mix, chicken strips, berries and peach in salad bowl.

- Toss with just enough salad dressing to coat salad. Put on 7-grain bread or serve on a bed of lettuce with bread, crackers or breadsticks. Serves 4.

Wrap-That-Turkey Burger

1 pound ground turkey	280 g
⅓ cup shredded 4-cheese blend	40 g
¼ cup finely grated, drained onion	40 g
1 teaspoon Creole spicy seasoning	5 ml

- Combine turkey, cheese, onion and spicy seasoning in bowl.

- Shape into 4 patties (make patties a little longer than round) and refrigerate about 30 minutes before cooking.

- Grill patties about 5 inches (13 cm) from heat for about 8 minutes or until thermometer reads 165° (70° C).

Wrap:

4 fajita-size flour tortillas, warmed	
2 cups shredded lettuce	70 g
⅔ cup prepared guacamole	150 g

- Place tortillas on flat surface and arrange one-fourth lettuce on each tortilla. Place 1 patty on each tortilla and spread with guacamole. Fold tortilla in half to cover filling. Serves 4.

TIP: If you don't want to buy spicy seasoning, use 1 teaspoon (5 ml) seasoned salt and ¼ teaspoon (1 ml) cayenne pepper.

BLT Tortilla Wraps

Flour tortillas
Mayonnaise
Sliced turkey
Cooked bacon
Shredded lettuce
Tomatoes, chopped

- Spread each tortilla with mayonnaise. Add 2 slices turkey, 2 slices bacon and shredded lettuce and tomatoes.

- Fold edges over to enclose filling. Serve immediately or wrap in wax paper and refrigerate.

Walnut-Cream Sandwiches

2 (8 ounce) packages cream cheese, softened	2 (225 g)
½ cup mayonnaise	110 g
1 teaspoon dijon-style mustard	5 ml
6 slices bacon, cooked, crumbled	
¾ cup finely chopped walnuts	65 g
Pumpernickel or rye bread	

- Beat cream cheese, mayonnaise and mustard in bowl until creamy. Fold in bacon and walnuts and mix well.

- Spread on pumpernickel or rye bread and slice in thirds. Serves 6.

Crab-Avocado Burgers

4 frozen crab cakes
1 ripe avocado
¼ cup mayonnaise   55 g
1 tablespoon lemon juice   5 ml
1 (4 ounce) can green
    chilies, drained   115 g
4 hamburger buns
Lettuce
Tomatoes

- Microwave crab cakes according to package directions. Mash avocado, mayonnaise, lemon juice and ½ teaspoon (2 ml) salt in bowl with fork. Stir in green chilies.

- Place crab cakes on buns and spread with avocado-mayonnaise mixture. Serve as is or top with lettuce and sliced tomatoes. Serves 4.

Hot Bunwiches

8 hamburger buns
8 slices Swiss cheese
8 slices deli ham
8 slices deli turkey
8 slices American cheese

- Lay out all 8 buns and place slices of Swiss cheese, ham, turkey and American cheese on bottom buns.

- Place top bun over American cheese, wrap each bunwich individually in foil and place in freezer. Remove from freezer 2 to 3 hours before serving.

- When ready to heat, preheat oven to 325° (160° C).

- Heat for about 30 minutes and serve hot. Serves 8.

Seafood Tortilla Wraps

2 large (9 inch) garden
   spinach tortillas   2 (23 cm)
Mayonnaise

- Heat broiler, place tortillas on baking sheet and broil very briefly on each side.

- Remove from oven and spread mayonnaise on 1 side of tortilla.

Filling:

1 cup shredded American
   cheese   115 g
1 (9 ounce) spring salad
   mix   255 g
1 cup diced tomatoes,
   drained   255 g
4 green onions, finely
   chopped
1 (4 ounce) package
  albacore tuna steak
  with lemon and
  cracked pepper,
  crumbled   115 g

- Spread cheese over tortillas and return to oven just until cheese melts.

- Combine salad mix, tomatoes and green onions in bowl and sprinkle on tortillas.

- Place as much of crumbled albacore on tortilla as needed.

- Roll or fold over to eat.
Serves 2

A tortilla is a flat bread made from corn or wheat flour.

Salmon Burgers

Salmon Patties:

1 (15 ounce) can salmon
   with liquid   425 g
1 egg, slightly beaten
2 tablespoons lemon juice 30 ml
⅔ cup seasoned
   breadcrumbs   80 g

Burgers:

Hamburger buns
Mayonnaise
Lettuce
Sliced tomatoes

- Combine salmon with
  2 tablespoons (30 ml) liquid
  from salmon can, egg, lemon
  juice, breadcrumbs and a little
  salt and pepper in bowl.

- Form into patties and fry with
  a little oil in skillet both sides
  until golden. Serve hot on buns
  with mayonnaise, lettuce and
  sliced tomatoes. Serve 6.

Fish and Chips Sandwiches

1 (12 ounce) box frozen
   breaded fish fillets,
   thawed   340 g
1 (16 ounce) loaf Italian
   bread   455 g
1 cup deli coleslaw   125 g
4 ounces potato chips   30 g

- Heat fish fillets according to
  package directions. Remove
  from oven and preheat broiler.
  Slice bread in half lengthwise
  and broil, cut-side up.

- Layer coleslaw, fish fillets and
  potato chips and cover with
  bread tops. To serve, cut into
  4 quarters and serve
  immediately. Serve 4.

Savory
Soups & Stews

Cheeses, Beans, Veggies, Greens and Meats

Savory Soups & Stews Contents

It is best to check your seasonings after cooking.
Sometimes the flavors may cook out over long periods
of time and you may need to add some seasonings again.

The Ultimate Cheddar Cheese Soup

1 cup finely chopped onion	160 g
1 red bell pepper, diced	
2 tablespoons butter	30 g
1 (16 ounce) package shredded extra sharp cheddar cheese	455 g
2 tablespoons cornstarch	15 g
1 (14 ounce) can chicken broth	400 g
1½ cups cooked, diced ham	210 g
1½ cups cooked broccoli florets	105 g
¾ cup cooked, diced carrots	95 g
1 teaspoon Worcestershire sauce	5 ml
½ teaspoon garlic powder	2 ml
1 (1 pint) carton half-and-half cream	500 ml

- Saute onion and bell pepper in butter in large saucepan. Mix cheese and cornstarch in bowl. Pour broth into saucepan and add cheese-cornstarch mixture a little at a time.

- Cook soup over medium heat until cheese melts. Stir until smooth and creamy.

- Add ham, broccoli, carrots, Worcestershire, garlic powder and a little salt and pepper and stir well. Heat over low heat, pour in half-and-half cream and stir well. Serves 6 to 8.

Easy Spinach Soup

2 (10 ounce) packages
   frozen chopped
   spinach, cooked   2 (280 g)
2 (10 ounce) cans
   cream of
   mushroom soup   2 (280 g)
1 cup half-and-half
   cream   310 g
1 (14 ounce) can
   chicken broth   400 g

- Place spinach, mushroom soup and half-and-half cream in blender and puree until smooth.

- Place spinach mixture and chicken broth in saucepan and heat on medium heat until hot.

- Reduce heat to low and simmer for 20 minutes. Serve hot or cold. Serve 6.

Speedy Creamy Broccoli-Rice Soup

1 (6 ounce) package
   chicken-flavored
   wild rice mix   170 g
1 (10 ounce) package
   chopped broccoli   280 g
2 (10 ounce) cans
   cream of chicken
   soup   2 (280 g)
1 (12 ounce) can
   chicken breast
   chunks   340 g

- Combine rice mix, seasoning packet and 5 cups (1.2 L) water in soup pot. Bring to a boil, reduce heat and simmer for 15 minutes.

- Stir in broccoli, chicken soup and chicken. Cover and simmer for additional 5 minutes. Serves 6.

Mexican-Style Minestrone Soup

1 (16 ounce) package frozen garlic-seasoned pasta and vegetables	455 g
1 (16 ounce) jar thick-and-chunky salsa	455 g
1 (15 ounce) can pinto beans with liquid	425 g
1 teaspoon chili powder	5 ml
1 teaspoon cumin	5 ml
1 (8 ounce) package shredded Mexican 4-cheese blend	230 g

- Combine pasta and vegetables, salsa, pinto beans, chili powder, cumin and 1 cup (250 ml) water in large saucepan.

- Heat to boiling, reduce heat to medium-low and simmer for about 8 minutes, stirring occasionally or until vegetables are tender. When ready to serve, top each serving with Mexican cheese. Serves 6.

Fiesta Soup

1 (15 ounce) can Mexican stewed tomatoes	425 g
1 (15 ounce) can whole kernel corn	425 g
1 (15 ounce) can pinto beans	425 g
1 (14 ounce) can chicken broth	400 g
1 (10 ounce) can fiesta nacho soup	280 g

- Combine tomatoes, corn, pinto beans, chicken broth and a little salt in soup pot on high heat and mix well.

- Stir in nacho soup and heat just until thoroughly hot. If you feel the soup needs a touch of meat, just add 1 (12 ounce/340 g) can white chicken chunks. Serves 6.

Black Bean Soup

2 (14 ounce) cans
    chicken broth   2 (400 g)
3 (15 ounce) cans
    black beans, rinsed
    and drained   3 (425 g)
2 (10 ounce) cans
    tomatoes and
    green chilies   2 (280 g)
1 onion, chopped
1 teaspoon ground
    cumin   5 ml
½ teaspoon dried
    thyme   2 ml
½ teaspoon dried
    oregano   2 ml
2 - 3 cups cooked,
    finely diced ham   280 - 420 g

- Combine chicken broth and black beans in slow cooker and turn cooker to HIGH. Cook just long enough for ingredients to get hot.

- With potato masher, mash about half of beans in slow cooker. Reduce heat to LOW and add tomatoes and green chilies, onion, spices, ham and ¾ cup (175 ml) water.

- Cover and cook for 5 to 6 hours. Serves 4 to 6.

Fresh chopped parsley added in the last few minutes of cooking adds a wonderful fresh flavor to soups and stews.

Navy Bean Soup

8 slices thick-cut bacon, divided
1 carrot
3 (15 ounce) cans navy beans with liquid   **3 (425 g)**
3 ribs celery, chopped
1 onion, chopped
2 (14 ounce) cans chicken broth   **2 (400 g)**
1 teaspoon Italian herb seasoning   **5 ml**
1 (10 ounce) can cream of chicken soup   **280 g**

- Cook bacon in skillet, drain and crumble. Reserve 2 crumbled slices for garnish. Cut carrot in half lengthwise and slice.

- Combine most of crumbled bacon, carrot, beans, celery, onion, broth, seasoning, 1 cup (250 ml) water in 5 to 6-quart (5 to 6 L) slow cooker and stir to mix.

- Cover and cook on LOW for 5 to 6 hours. Ladle 2 cups (500 ml) soup mixture into food processor or blender and process until smooth.

- Return to cooker, add cream of chicken soup and stir to mix. Turn heat to HIGH and cook for additional 10 to 15 minutes. Serves 4 to 6.

Easy Meaty Minestrone

2 (20 ounce) cans
    minestrone soup   2 (570 g)
1 (15 ounce) can pinto
    beans with juice   425 g
1 (18 ounce) package
    frozen Italian
    meatballs, thawed 510 g
1 (5 ounce) package
    grated parmesan
    cheese   145 g

- Combine soups, beans, meatballs and ½ cup (125 ml) water in large saucepan.

- Bring to a boil, reduce heat to low and simmer for about 15 minutes. To serve, sprinkle each serving with parmesan cheese. Serve 6 to 8.

Mexican Black Bean Soup

2 onions, finely chopped
Canola oil
3 teaspoons minced
    garlic   15 ml
3 teaspoons chili
    powder   15 ml
3 (15 ounce) cans
    black beans   3 (425 g)
1 teaspoon cumin   5 ml
1 (14 ounce) can
    beef broth   400 g
Shredded cheese or
    salsa

- Saute onions in soup pot with little oil and cook on medium heat for 5 minutes. Stir in garlic and chili powder.

- Puree 1 can beans and add to onion mixture. Add remaining beans, cumin and beef broth.

- Bring to a boil, reduce heat and simmer for 10 minutes. When serving, garnish with shredded cheese or salsa. Serves 4.

Southern Turnip Greens Stew

2 (16 ounce) packages
    frozen chopped
    turnip greens   2 (455 g)
1 (10 ounce) package
    frozen diced onions
    and bell peppers   280 g
2 cups cooked,
    chopped ham   280 g
1 teaspoon sugar   5 ml
2 (14 ounce) cans
    chicken broth   2 (400 g)

- Combine turnip greens, onions
  and bell peppers, ham, sugar,
  chicken broth and

- 1 teaspoon (5 ml) black pepper
  in soup pot.

- Boil mixture, reduce heat, cover
  and simmer for 30 minutes.
  Serves 6.

Tater Talk Soup

5 medium potatoes,
    peeled, cubed
2 cups cooked, cubed
    ham   280 g
1 cup fresh broccoli
    florets, cut very,
    very fine   70 g
1 (10 ounce) can cheddar
    cheese soup   280 g
1 (10 ounce) can fiesta
    nacho cheese soup   280 g
1 (14 ounce) can
    chicken broth   400 g
2½ soup cans milk   625 g
Paprika

- Place potatoes, ham and broccoli
  in sprayed slow cooker.

- Combine soups, broth and milk
  in saucepan. Heat just enough
  to mix until smooth. Stir into
  slow cooker. Cover and cook on
  LOW for 7 to 9 hours.

- When serving, sprinkle a little
  paprika over each serving, if
  desired. Serves 6.

Southern Soup

1½ cups dry black-eyed
   peas   295 g
2 - 3 cups cooked,
   diced ham   280 - 420 g
1 (15 ounce) can
   whole kernel corn 425 g
1 (10 ounce) package
   frozen cut okra,
   thawed   280 g
1 onion, chopped
1 large potato, cubed
2 teaspoons Cajun
   seasoning   10 ml
1 (14 ounce) can
   chicken broth   400 g
2 (15 ounce) cans
   Mexican stewed
   tomatoes   2 (425 g)

- Rinse peas and drain. Combine peas and 5 cups (1.2 L) water in large saucepan. Bring to a boil, reduce heat, simmer for about 10 minutes and drain.

- Combine peas, ham, corn, okra, onion, potato, seasoning, broth and 2 cups (500 ml) water in 5 or 6-quart (5 or 6 L) slow cooker.

- Cover and cook on LOW for 6 to 8 hours. Add stewed tomatoes and continue cooking for additional 1 hour. Serves 6.

To make a good base for your soup, you can use any of the following: canned soups (such as cream of mushroom soup), canned tomatoes, tomato juice, canned chicken broth, homemade stocks, commercial soup bases, clam or seafood broth, or bacon for extra flavor.

Corn-Ham Chowder

1 (14 ounce) can
chicken broth   400 g
1 cup milk   250 ml
1 (10 ounce) can
cream of celery
soup   280 g
1 (15 ounce) can
cream-style corn   425 g
1 (15 ounce) can
whole kernel corn   425 g
½ cup dry potato
flakes   30 g
1 onion, chopped
2 - 3 cups cooked,
chopped, ham   280 - 420 g

- Combine broth, milk, soup, cream-style corn, whole kernel corn, potato flakes, onion and ham in 6-quart (6 L) slow cooker.

- Cover and cook on LOW for 4 to 5 hours. When ready to serve, season with a little salt and black pepper. Serves 6.

Easy Pork Tenderloin Stew

This is a great recipe for leftover pork or beef.

2 - 3 cups cooked,
cubed pork   280 - 420 g
1 (12 ounce) jar pork
gravy   340 g
¼ cup chili sauce   70 g
1 (16 ounce) package
frozen stew
vegetables   455 g
Cornbread or hot
biscuits

- Combine pork, gravy, chili sauce, stew vegetables and ½ cup (125 ml) water in soup pot.

- Bring to a boil and boil for 2 minutes; reduce heat and simmer for 10 minutes. Serve with cornbread or hot biscuits. Serves 4.

Ham-Vegetable Chowder

This is a great recipe for leftover ham.

1 medium potato
2 (10 ounce) cans
   cream of celery
   soup   2 (280 g)
1 (14 ounce) can
   chicken broth   400 g
2 cups cooked, finely
   diced ham   280 g
1 (15 ounce) can
   whole kernel corn   425 g

2 carrots, sliced
1 onion, coarsely
   chopped
1 teaspoon dried
   basil   5 ml
1 (10 ounce) package
   frozen broccoli
   florets   280 g

- Cut potato into 1-inch (2.5 cm) pieces. Combine all ingredients except broccoli florets in large slow cooker.

- Cover and cook on LOW for 5 to 6 hours. Add broccoli, about ½ teaspoon (2 ml) each of salt and pepper to cooker and cook for additional 1 hour. Serves 4.

The word chowder comes from the French word "chaudiere," a caldron in which fishermen made their stews fresh from the sea. Chowder is a thick, chunky seafood or other thick, rich soup containing chunky food.

Easy Potato Soup

1 (18 ounce) package frozen hash-brown potatoes	510 g
1 cup chopped onion	160 g
1 (14 ounce) can chicken broth	400 g
1 (10 ounce) can cream of celery soup	280 g
1 (10 ounce) can cream of chicken soup	280 g
2 cups milk	500 ml

- Combine potatoes, onion and 2 cups (500 ml) water in large saucepan and bring to a boil.

- Cover, reduce heat and simmer for 30 minutes.

- Stir in broth, soups and milk and heat thoroughly. (If you like, garnish with shredded cheddar cheese or cooked, diced ham.) Serves 6.

Potato-Sausage Soup

1 pound pork sausage links	455 g
1 cup chopped celery	100 g
1 cup chopped onion	160 g
2 (10 ounce) cans potato soup	2 (280 g)
2 (14 ounce) cans chicken broth	2 (400 g)

- Cut sausage in 1-inch (2.5 cm) slices.

- Brown sausage slices in large heavy skillet, drain and remove sausage to separate bowl.

- Leave about 2 tablespoons (30 ml) sausage drippings in skillet and saute celery and onion.

- Add potato soup, ¾ cup (175 ml) water, chicken broth and cooked sausage slices. Bring to a boil, reduce heat and simmer for 20 minutes. Serves 6.

Black Bean Stew Supper

1 (16 ounce) pork and beef sausage ring, thinly sliced	455 g
2 onions, chopped	
3 ribs celery, chopped	
Canola oil	
3 (15 ounce) cans black beans, drained, rinsed	3 (425 g)
2 (10 ounce) cans diced tomatoes and green chilies	2 (280 g)
2 (14 ounce) cans chicken broth	2 (400 g)

- Place sausage slices, onion and celery in soup pot with a little oil and cook until sausage is slightly brown and onion is soft. Drain and discard fat.

- Add beans, tomatoes and green chilies and broth. Bring mixture to a boil, reduce heat and simmer for 30 minutes.

- Take out about 2 to 3 cups (500 to 750 ml) soup mixture, place in blender and pulse until almost smooth. Return mixture to soup pot and stir to thicken stew.

- Return heat to high until stew is thoroughly hot. Serves 6.

Need to thicken your soup? Adding a little pasta or mashed potato flakes is a great way to add body to your soup.

Polish Vegetable Stew

Canola oil
1 onion, sliced
1 carrot, sliced
2 (15 ounce) cans
    stewed tomatoes   2 (425 g)
1 pound Polish
    sausage   455 g
2 (15 ounce) cans
    new potatoes,
    quartered   2 (425 g)
1 (9 ounce) package
    coleslaw mix   255 g

- Place a little oil in large soup pot. Cook onion and carrot slices for 3 minutes or until tender-crisp and add tomatoes.

- Cut sausage in 1-inch (2.5 cm) pieces. Add potatoes and sausage to soup mixture.

- Bring to a boil, reduce heat and simmer for 10 minutes.

- Stir in coleslaw mix, cook for additional 8 minutes and stir occasionally. Serves 6.

Italian Garbanzo Bean Soup

1 (16 ounce) package
    frozen diced onions
    and bell peppers   455 g
Canola oil
1 pound Italian
    sausages, sliced   455 g
1 (14 ounce) can beef
    broth   400 g
1 (15 ounce) can
    Italian stewed
    tomatoes   425 g
2 (15 ounce) cans
    garbanzo beans
    (chickpeas),
    rinsed, drained   2 (425 g)

- Saute onions and bell peppers in soup pot with a little oil. Add Italian sausage and cook until brown. Stir in beef broth, stewed tomatoes and garbanzo beans.

- Bring mixture to a boil, reduce heat and simmer for about 30 minutes. Serves 6.

Quick Spicy Tomato Soup

2 (10 ounce) cans
   tomato soup   2 (280 g)
1 (15 ounce) can
   Mexican stewed
   tomatoes   425 g
Sour cream
½ pound bacon,
   fried, drained,
   crumbled   230 g

- Combine soup and stewed tomatoes in saucepan and heat.

- To serve, place dollop of sour cream on top of soup and sprinkle crumbled bacon over sour cream. Serves 4.

Spaghetti Soup

1 (7 ounce) package
   precut spaghetti   200 g
1 (18 ounce) package
   frozen, cooked
   meatballs, thawed   510 g
1 (28 ounce) jar spaghetti
   sauce   795 g
1 (15 ounce) can Mexican
   stewed tomatoes   425 g

- In soup pot with 3 quarts (3 L) boiling water and a little salt, cook spaghetti in soup pot with 3 quarts (3 L) boiling water for about 6 minutes (no need to drain).

- When spaghetti is done, add meatballs, spaghetti sauce and stewed tomatoes and cook until mixture heats through. Serves 6.

TIP: To garnish each soup bowl, sprinkle with 2 tablespoons (15 g) mozzarella cheese or whatever cheese you have in the refrigerator.

Spicy Sausage Soup

1 pound mild bulk sausage	455 g
1 pound hot bulk sausage	455 g
2 (15 ounce) cans Mexican stewed tomatoes	2 (425 g)
3 cups chopped celery	305 g
1 cup sliced carrots	120 g
1 (15 ounce) can cut green beans, drained	425 g
1 (14 ounce) can chicken broth	400 g
1 teaspoon seasoned salt	5 ml

- Combine mild and hot sausage, shape into small balls and place in non-stick skillet.

- Brown thoroughly and drain. Place in large slow cooker.

- Add remaining ingredients plus 1 teaspoon (5 ml) salt and 1 cup (250 ml) water Stir gently so meatballs will not break up.

- Cover and cook on LOW for 6 to 7 hours. Serves 6.

If your sauce, soup or stew is too salty, add a peeled potato to the pot and it will absorb the extra salt. You can also add some potato flakes if you have them.

Enchilada Soup

1 pound lean ground
   beef, browned,
   drained   455 g
1 (15 ounce) can
   Mexican stewed
   tomatoes   425 g
1 (15 ounce) can pinto
   beans with liquid   425 g
1 (15 ounce) can
   whole kernel corn,
   with liquid   425 g
1 onion, chopped
2 (10 ounce) cans
   enchilada sauce   2 (280 g)
1 (8 ounce) package
   shredded 4-cheese
   blend   230 g
Tortilla chips, crushed

- Combine beef, tomatoes, beans, corn, onion, enchilada sauce and 1 cup (250 ml) water in sprayed 5 to 6 (5 to 6 L) slow cooker and mix well.

- Cover and cook on LOW for 6 to 8 hours or on HIGH for 3 to 4 hours.

- Stir in shredded cheese. If desired, top each serving with a few crushed tortilla chips. Serves 6.

Did you know ice cubes love fat? If you drop a few cubes into your soup, fat will cling to them and it's easy to remove it.

Mexican Meatball Soup

3 (14 ounce) cans
   beef broth   3 (400 g)
1 (16 ounce) jar hot
   salsa   455 g
1 (16 ounce) package
   frozen whole
   kernel corn,
   thawed   455 g
1 (16 ounce) package
   frozen meatballs,
   thawed   455 g
1 teaspoon minced
   garlic   5 ml

- Combine all ingredients in slow cooker and stir well.

- Cover and cook on LOW for 4 to 7 hours. Serve 6.

Beefy Vegetable Soup

1 pound lean ground beef 455 g
1 (46 ounce) can cocktail
   vegetable juice   1.4 L
1 (1 ounce) packet onion
   soup mix   30 g
1 (3 ounce) package
   beef-flavored
   ramen noodles   85 g
1 (16 ounce) package
   frozen mixed
   vegetables   455 g

- Brown beef in large soup pot over medium heat and drain. Stir in cocktail juice, soup mix, contents of noodle seasoning packet and mixed vegetables.

- Heat mixture to boiling, reduce heat and simmer for 6 minutes or until vegetables are tender-crisp. Return to boiling, stir in noodles and cook for 3 minutes. Serves 6.

Hamburger Soup

2 pounds lean ground beef	910 g
2 (15 ounce) cans chili without beans	2 (425 g)
1 (16 ounce) package frozen mixed vegetables, thawed	455 g
3 (14 ounce) cans beef broth	3 (400 g)
2 (15 ounce) cans stewed tomatoes	2 (425 g)

- Brown ground beef in skillet and place in 6-quart (6 L) slow cooker.

- Add chili, vegetables, broth, tomatoes, 1 cup (250 ml) water and 1 teaspoon (5 ml) salt and stir well. Cover and cook on LOW for 6 to 7 hours. Serves 6.

Taco Soup

1½ pounds lean ground beef	680 g
1 (1 ounce) packet taco seasoning	30 g
2 (15 ounce) cans Mexican stewed tomatoes	2 (425 g)
2 (15 ounce) cans chili beans with liquid	2 (425 g)
1 (15 ounce) can whole kernel corn, drained	425 g
Tortilla chips, crushed	
Shredded cheddar cheese	

- Brown ground beef in skillet and place in 5 to 6-quart (5 to 6 L) slow cooker. Add taco seasoning, tomatoes, chili beans, corn and 1 cup (250 ml) water and mix well.

- Cover and cook on LOW for 4 hours or on HIGH for 1 to 2 hours. Serve over crushed tortilla chips and sprinkle some shredded cheddar cheese over top of each serving. Serves 6.

Taco Soup Olé

2 pounds lean ground beef	910 g
2 (15 ounce) cans ranch-style beans with liquid	2 (425 g)
1 (15 ounce) can whole kernel corn, drained	425 g
2 (15 ounce) cans stewed tomatoes	2 (425 g)
1 (10 ounce) can tomatoes and green chilies	280 g
1 (1 ounce) packet ranch-style dressing mix	30 g
1 (1 ounce) packet taco seasoning	30 g

- Brown ground beef in large skillet, drain and transfer to slow cooker.

- Add remaining ingredients and stir well. Cover and cook on LOW for 8 to 10 hours. Serves 6.

TIP: For a nice touch, sprinkle shredded cheddar cheese over each serving.

A real time-saver is to make a large pot of soup or stew and divide it into serving portions in resealable plastic bags. Freeze enough for one, two or four. When the bag is sealed, it will lie flat in the freezer and won't take up as much room as containers. Be sure to leave a little room for expansion as it freezes.

Meatball Stew I

1 (18 ounce) package
   frozen Italian
   meatballs   510 g
1 (14 ounce) cans
   beef broth   400 g
2 (15 ounce) cans
   Italian stewed
   tomatoes   2 (425 g)
1 (16 ounce) package
   frozen stew
   vegetables   455 g

- Place meatballs, beef broth and stewed tomatoes in large saucepan. Bring to boiling, reduce heat and simmer for 10 minutes or until meatballs are thoroughly hot.

- Add vegetables and cook on medium heat for 10 minutes. Mixture will be fairly thin. Serves 6.

TIP: If you like thicker stew, thicken this by mixing 2 tablespoons (15 g) cornstarch in ¼ cup (60 ml) water and stir into stew, bring to boiling and stir constantly until stew thickens.

Meatball Stew II

1 (18 ounce) package
   frozen Italian
   meatballs, thawed 510 g
1 (14 ounce) can
   beef broth   400 g
1 (15 ounce) can cut
   green beans   425 g
1 (16 ounce) package
   baby carrots   455 g
2 (15 ounce) cans
   stewed tomatoes 2 (425 g)
1 tablespoon
   Worcestershire sauce
   15 ml
½ teaspoon ground
   allspice   2 ml

- Combine all ingredients in slow cooker. Cover and cook on LOW for 3 to 5 hours. Serves 6.

Quick
Brunswick Stew

This is great with cornbread!

1 (15 ounce) can	
beef stew	425 g
1 (15 ounce) can	
chicken stew	425 g
1 (15 ounce) can lima	
beans	425 g
2 (15 ounce) cans	
stewed tomatoes	2 (425 g)
1 (15 ounce) can	
whole kernel	
corn, drained	425 g
½ teaspoon hot	
sauce, optional	2 ml

- Combine beef stew, chicken stew, beans, tomatoes and corn in large stew pot. Bring stew to a boil on medium-high heat, reduce heat and simmer for 35 minutes. Serves 6.

TIP: Brunswick stew needs to be a little spicy, so stir in hot sauce. If you don't want the "spicy", add 1 tablespoon (15 ml) Worcestershire sauce to the stew.

When you're pouring soup or stew from one container to another, pour it over the back of a large spoon. The spoon will reduce the splatter and the process will have less cleanup.

Chicken-Pasta Soup

1½ pounds boneless, skinless chicken thighs, boned, cubed	680 g
1 onion, chopped	
3 carrots, sliced	
½ cup halved pitted ripe olives	65 g
1 teaspoon prepared minced garlic	5 ml
3 (14 ounce) cans chicken broth	3 (400 g)
1 (15 ounce) can Italian stewed tomatoes	425 g
1 teaspoon Italian seasoning	5 ml
½ cup small shell pasta	40 g
Parmesan cheese	

- Combine all ingredients except shell pasta and parmesan cheese in slow cooker.

- Cover and cook on LOW for 8 to 9 hours. About 30 minutes before serving, add pasta and stir.

- Increase heat to HIGH and cook for additional 20 to 30 minutes. Serve with parmesan cheese. Serves 6.

If you cook your pasta before adding it to your soup, it doesn't bring all the starch with it and can be added last so it doesn't get overcooked. You can even use leftover pasta that you have in the refrigerator.

White Lightning Chili

3 (15 ounce) cans
   navy beans with
   liquid   3 (425 g)
3 (14 ounce) cans
   chicken broth   3 (400 g)
1 (10 ounce) can
   cream of chicken
   soup   280 g
2 tablespoons butter,
   melted   30 g
2 onions, chopped
3 cups cooked,
   chopped chicken
   or turkey   420 g
1 (7 ounce) can
   chopped green
   chilies   200 g
1 teaspoon minced
   garlic   5 ml
½ teaspoon dried
   basil   2 ml
½ teaspoon
   white pepper   2 ml
⅛ teaspoon cayenne
   pepper   .5 ml
⅛ teaspoon ground
   cloves   .5 ml
1 teaspoon ground
   oregano   5 ml
1 (8 ounce) package
   shredded 4-cheese
   blend   230 g

- Combine all ingredients
  except cheese in slow cooker.
  Cover and cook on LOW for
  4 to 5 hours.

- When serving, sprinkle cheese
  over top of each serving.
  Serves 6.

Country Chicken Chowder

1½ pounds boneless, skinless chicken breast halves	680 g
2 tablespoons butter	30 g
2 (10 ounce) cans cream of potato soup	2 (280 g)
1 (14 ounce) can chicken broth	400 g
1 (8 ounce) package frozen whole kernel corn	230 g
1 onion, sliced	
2 ribs celery, sliced	
1 (10 ounce) package frozen peas and carrots, thawed	280 g
½ teaspoon dried thyme leaves	2 ml
½ cup half-and-half cream	155 g

- Cut chicken into 1-inch (2.5 cm) strips.

- Brown chicken strips in butter in skillet and transfer to large slow cooker.

- Add soup, broth, corn, onion, celery, peas and carrots, and thyme and stir.

- Cover and cook on LOW for 3 to 4 hours or until vegetables are tender. Turn off heat, stir in half-and-half cream and set aside for about 10 minutes before serving. Serves 6.

Americans consume more than 10 billion bowls of soup every year.

Confetti Chicken Soup

1 pound skinless,
  boneless chicken
  thighs   455 g
1 (6 ounce) package
  chicken and
  herb-flavored rice 170 g
3 (14 ounce) cans
  chicken broth   3 (400 g)
3 carrots, sliced
1 (10 ounce) can
  cream of chicken
  soup   280 g
1½ tablespoons
  chicken seasoning 22 ml
1 (10 ounce) package
  frozen whole
  kernel corn,
  thawed   280 g
1 (10 ounce) package
  frozen baby green
  peas, thawed   280 g

- Cut thighs in thin strips. Combine chicken, rice, broth, carrots, soup, seasoning and 1 cup (250 ml) water in 5 to 6-quart (5 to 6 L) slow cooker.

- Cover and cook on LOW for 8 to 9 hours.

- About 30 minutes before serving, turn heat to high and add corn and peas to cooker. Continue cooking for additional 30 minutes. Serves 6.

Use frozen vegetables such as peas, spinach or corn to cut prep time when making soup. Add them to assorted soups or puree them with broth, cream and sauteed onion and simmer to make a smooth soup.

Tasty Turkey Soup

1 (16 ounce) package
   frozen chopped
   onions and bell
   peppers   455 g
Canola oil
2 (3 ounce) packages
   chicken-flavored
   ramen noodles   2 (85 g)
2 (10 ounce) cans
   cream of chicken
   soup   2 (280 g)
1 cup leftover cubed
   turkey   140 g

- Cook onions and bell peppers in soup pot with a little oil just until tender but not brown. Add ramen noodles, seasoning packet and 2 cups (500 ml) water. Cook for 5 minutes or until noodles are tender.

- Stir in chicken soup and turkey. Heat, stirring constantly until thoroughly hot. Serves 6.

So Easy Peanut Soup

2 (10 ounce) cans
   cream of chicken
   soup   2 (280 g)
2 soups cans milk
1¼ cups crunchy
   peanut butter   360 g

- Blend soup and milk in saucepan on medium heat.

- Stir in peanut butter and heat until it blends. Serve hot. Serves 4.

Chicken-Noodle Soup

1 (3 ounce) package chicken-flavored ramen noodles, broken	85 g
1 (10 ounce) package frozen green peas, thawed	280 g
1 (4 ounce) jar sliced mushrooms	115 g
3 cups cooked, cubed chicken	420 g

- Heat 2¼ cups (560 ml) water to boiling in large saucepan and add ramen noodles, contents of seasoning packet and peas.

- (It's even better if you add 2 tablespoons (30 g) butter.)

- Heat to a boil; reduce heat to medium and cook for about 5 minutes.

- Stir in mushrooms, chicken and ¾ teaspoon (4 ml) pepper and continue cooking over medium heat until all ingredients heat through. Serves 6.

TIP: Garnish with about 1 cup (55 g) lightly crushed potato chips, if desired.

A team of scientists at the University of Nebraska confirms what grandmothers have known for centuries – that chicken soup is good for colds. Chicken soup contains several anti-inflammatory ingredients that affect the immune system.

Tasty Chicken and Rice Soup

1 pound boneless skinless chicken breasts	455 g
½ cup brown rice	185 g
1 (10 ounce) can cream of chicken soup	280 g
1 (10 ounce) can cream of celery soup	280 g
1 (14 ounce) can chicken broth with roasted garlic	400 g
1 (16 ounce) package frozen sliced carrots, thawed	455 g
1 cup half-and-half cream	310 g

- Cut chicken into 1-inch (2.5 cm) pieces.

- Place pieces in sprayed 4 to 5-quart (4 to 5 L) slow cooker.

- Mix rice, soups, chicken broth and carrots in bowl and pour over chicken.

- Cover and cook on LOW for 7 to 8 hours.

- Turn heat to HIGH, add half-and-half cream and cook for additional 15 to 20 minutes. Serves 6.

A wire whisk is super for blending canned soups and water.

Tortellini Soup

1 (1 ounce) packet white sauce mix	30 g
3 boneless, skinless chicken breast halves	
1 (14 ounce) can chicken broth	400 g
1 teaspoon minced garlic	5 ml
½ teaspoon dried basil	2 ml
½ teaspoon oregano	2 ml
½ teaspoon cayenne pepper	2 ml
1 (8 ounce) package cheese tortellini	230 g
1½ cups half-and-half cream	470 g
6 cups fresh baby spinach	180 g

- Place white sauce mix in sprayed 5 to 6 (5 to 6 L) slow cooker.

- Add 4 cups (1 L) water and stir until mixture is smooth. Cut chicken into 1-inch (2.5 cm) pieces.

- Add chicken, broth, garlic, ½ teaspoon (2 ml) salt, basil, oregano and cayenne pepper to mixture.

- Cover and cook on LOW for 6 to 7 hours or on HIGH for 3 hours.

- Stir in tortellini, cover and cook for additional 1 hour on HIGH.

- Stir in half-and-half cream and fresh spinach and cook just enough for soup to get hot. Serves 6.

TIP: Sprinkle a little shredded parmesan cheese on top of each serving as a nice touch.

In southern Italy, soup is said to relieve your hunger, quench your thirst, fill your stomach, clean your teeth, make you sleep, help you digest and color your cheeks.

Tortilla Soup

3 large boneless, skinless
   chicken breast halves,
   cubed
1 (10 ounce) package
   frozen whole
   kernel corn,
   thawed   280 g
1 onion, chopped
3 (14 ounce) cans
   chicken broth   3 (400 g)
1 (6 ounce) can
   tomato paste   170 g
2 (10 ounce) cans
   tomatoes and
   green chilies   2 (280 g)
2 teaspoons ground
   cumin   10 ml
1 teaspoon chili
   powder   5 ml
1 teaspoon seasoned
   salt   5 ml
1 teaspoon minced
   garlic   5 ml
6 corn tortillas

- Preheat oven to 375° (190° C).

- Combine chicken, corn, onion, broth, tomato paste, tomatoes and green chilies, cumin, chili powder, seasoned salt and garlic in large slow cooker.

- Cover and cook on LOW for 5 to 7 hours or on HIGH for 3 to 3 hours 30 minutes.

- While soup is cooking, cut tortillas into ¼-inch (6 mm) strips and place on baking sheet.

- Bake for about 5 minutes or until crisp.

- Serve baked tortilla strips with soup. Serves 6.

Big-Time Beef

Baked, Broiled, Fried, and Cooked Slow and Easy

Big-Time Beef Contents

Grilled Steak with Garlic-Mustard Sauce

⅓ cup apple juice	75 ml
2 tablespoons dijon-style mustard	30 g
1 tablespoon minced garlic	15 ml
4 (1 inch) thick boneless beef top strip steaks	4 (2.5 cm)

- Combine apple juice, mustard, garlic and 1 teaspoon (5 ml) black pepper in bowl, and mix well. Remove and reserve ¼ cup (60 ml) sauce for basting. Brush steaks with remaining sauce.

- Grill steaks on grill over medium hot coals. Grill for about 15 to 18 minutes or until desired doneness and turn occasionally.

- During last 8 to 10 minutes of grilling, baste steaks with the ¼ cup (60 ml) sauce set aside for basting. Serves 4.

When buying fillets or steaks, be sure the meat is uniform in color with no brown spots.

Marinated London Broil

1 (12 ounce) can cola	340 g
1 (10 ounce) bottle teriyaki sauce	280 g
1 (3 pound) London broil	1.4 kg

- Combine cola, teriyaki sauce and 1 teaspoon (5 ml) black pepper in large resealable plastic bag. Seal, marinate in refrigerator for 24 hours and turn occasionally.

- Remove London broil from marinade and discard marinade. Grill covered for about 14 minutes on each side.

- Let stand for about 10 minutes before slicing diagonally across grain. Serves 8.

Swiss Steak Supper

1 - 1½ pounds boneless, round steak	455 - 680 g
8 - 10 medium new (red) potatoes with peels, halved	
1 cup baby carrots	120 g
1 onion, sliced	
1 (15 ounce) can stewed tomatoes	425 g
1 (12 ounce) jar beef gravy	340 g

- Cut steak in 6 to 8 serving-size pieces, season with ½ teaspoon (2 ml) each of salt and pepper and brown in non-stick skillet. Layer steak pieces, potatoes, carrots and onion in slow cooker.

- Combine tomatoes and beef gravy in saucepan and spoon over vegetables. Cover and cook on LOW for 7 to 8 hours. Serves 6 to 8.

Steak and Potatoes

2 pounds round steak	910 g
⅓ cup flour	40 g
⅓ cup canola oil	75 ml
5 peeled potatoes, diced	
¼ cup chopped onions	40 g
1 (10 ounce) cream of mushroom soup	280 g

- Preheat oven to 350° (175° C).

- Cut steak in serving-size pieces and coat in flour. Brown with oil in heavy skillet and drain. Place steak in sprayed 9 x 13-inch (23 x 33 cm) baking dish.

- Season potatoes with a little salt and pepper, place over steak and cover with onions and mushroom soup diluted with ½ cup (125 ml) water. Cover and bake for 1 hour 30 minutes. Serves 8.

Skillet Steak and Veggies

1 pound boneless sirloin steak, cut in strips	455 g
Canola oil	
2 (15 ounce) cans Italian stewed tomatoes with juice	2 (425 g)
1 (16 ounce) package frozen Italian green beans, thawed	455 g
1 (8 ounce) carton sour cream	230 g
Noodles, cooked	

- Place sirloin strips in large skillet with a little oil. Cook on high heat for about 3 minutes.

- Add stewed tomatoes and green beans, bring to a boil, lower heat and cook for 10 minutes.

- Just before serving, fold in sour cream. Serve over noodles. Serves 6.

Zesty Rice and Beef

1 pound lean ground
   round steak   455 g
1 onion, chopped
1 green bell pepper,
   chopped
2½ cups cooked rice   415 g
1 (15 ounce) whole kernel
   corn, drained   425 g
1 (15 ounce) can Mexican
   stewed tomatoes   425 g
1 (15 ounce) can diced
   tomatoes   425 g
2 teaspoons chili powder   10 ml
1 teaspoon garlic powder   5 ml
1 (8 ounce) package
   cubed Velveeta®
   cheese   230 g
1 cup buttery cracker
   crumbs   60 g
½ cup chopped pecans
   or walnuts   55 g
2 tablespoons butter,
   melted   30 g

- Preheat oven to 350° (175° C).

- Cook beef, onion and bell pepper in large skillet or roasting pan over medium heat until beef is no longer pink. Drain well.

- Add rice, corn, stewed tomatoes, diced tomatoes, chili powder, garlic powder and ½ teaspoon (2 ml) teaspoon salt and bring to a boil. Remove from heat.

- Add cheese and stir until cheese melts. Spoon into sprayed 9 x 13-inch (23 x 33 cm) baking dish. Combine cracker crumbs, pecans and butter in bowl. Sprinkle over top of casserole. Bake for 25 minutes or until casserole is bubbly hot. Serves 8.

Thai Beef, Noodles and Veggies

2 (4.4 ounce) packages
   Thai sesame
   noodles   4 (130 g)
1 pound sirloin steak,
   cut in strips   455 g
Canola oil
1 (16 ounce) package
   frozen stir-fry
   vegetables, thawed 455 g
½ cup chopped
   peanuts   85 g

- Cook noodles according to package directions, remove from heat. Place in serving bowl, cover and keep warm.

- Season sirloin strips with a little salt and pepper.

- Brown half sirloin strips in a little oil in skillet and cook for about 2 minutes. Remove from skillet and drain.

- Add remaining sirloin strips, brown in skillet with a little oil and cook for about 2 minutes. Remove from skillet and drain.

- In same skillet, place vegetables and ½ cup (125 ml) water, cover and cook for 5 minutes or until tender-crisp.

- Remove from heat, add steak strips and toss to mix.

- Spoon over warm noodles to serve; sprinkle with peanuts. Serves 6.

Natural peanut butter is made without sugar or hydrogenated oils and has a thicker texture than regular peanut butter.

On-the-Border Steak

½ teaspoon dry mustard   2 ml
2 tablespoons fajita
    seasoning   30 ml
1 teaspoon minced garlic 5 ml
1½ pounds flank steak   680 g
Canola oil
1 cup chunky salsa,
    heated   265 g
Rice, cooked

- Combine ½ teaspoon (2 ml) pepper, dry mustard, fajita seasoning and garlic in bowl. Rub flank steak with a little oil, sprinkle seasonings over steak and refrigerate for 4 to 6 hours.

- Grill steak on each side on covered grill for 6 to 8 minutes on medium heat. Cut steak diagonally across grain into thin strips.

- Serve with hot salsa and spoon over rice. Serves 6.

Skillet Sirloin

2 teaspoons canola oil   10 ml
2 teaspoons minced garlic 10 ml
½ teaspoon cayenne
    pepper   2 ml
2 tablespoons soy sauce   30 ml
2 tablespoons honey   30 ml
1 pound beef sirloin,
    thinly sliced   455 g
Rice, cooked

- Combine oil, garlic, cayenne pepper, soy sauce and honey and place in resealable plastic bag.

- Add sliced beef, seal bag and shake. Refrigerate for 30 minutes.

- Place beef mixture in large sprayed skillet over medium-high heat. Cook for 5 to 6 minutes or until desired doneness, but do not over-cook. Serve over rice. Serves 6.

Seasoned-Beef Tenderloin

3 tablespoons dijon-style mustard	40 g
2 tablespoons horseradish	30 g
1 (3 pound) center-cut beef tenderloin	1.4 kg
½ cup seasoned breadcrumbs	60 g

- Combine mustard and horseradish in bowl and spread over beef tenderloin.

- Spread breadcrumbs onto horseradish-mustard mixture and wrap beef in foil. Refrigerate for at least 12 hours.

- When ready to bake, preheat oven to 375° (190° C).

- Remove wrap and place on sprayed broiler pan. Bake for 30 minutes. Let tenderloin stand for 15 minutes before slicing. Serves 8 to 10.

Steak with Creamy Horseradish Sauce

1 (2 pound) sirloin steak	910 g
1 (8 ounce) carton sour cream	230 g
¼ cup horseradish	60 g

- Preheat broiler. Pat steak dry and sprinkle liberally with salt and pepper.

- Broil steak on rack for about 3 inches (8 cm) from heat for about 5 minutes on both sides. Let stand for 5 minutes before slicing.

- Combine sour cream, horseradish and a little salt and pepper in bowl and mix well. Serve with sirloin steak. Serves 8.

Old-Time Pot Roast

1 (2 - 2½) pound
   boneless rump
   roast   **910 g - 1.1 kg**
5 medium potatoes,
   peeled, quartered
1 (16 ounce) package
   peeled baby
   carrots   **455 g**
2 medium onions,
   quartered
1 (10 ounce) can
   golden mushroom
   soup   **280 g**
½ teaspoon dried
   basil   **2 ml**

- Brown roast in skillet on all sides. Place potatoes, carrots and onions in sprayed 4 to 5-quart (4 to 5 L) slow cooker.

- Place browned roast on top of vegetables.

- Combine soup, basil and ½ teaspoon (2 ml) salt in bowl and pour mixture over meat and vegetables.

- Cover and cook on LOW for 9 to 11 hours. Serves 8.

TIP: To serve, transfer roast and vegetables to serving plate. Stir juices remaining in slow cooker and spoon over roast and vegetables.

O'Brian's Hash

3 cups cubed, cooked
  beef roast   420 g
1 (28 ounce) package
  frozen hash browns
  with onions and
  peppers, thawed   795 g
Canola oil
1 (16 ounce) jar salsa   455 g
1 tablespoon beef
  seasoning   15 ml
1 cup shredded
  cheddar-Jack cheese   115 g

- Place cubed beef in large, sprayed slow cooker.

- Brown potatoes in a little oil in large skillet and transfer to slow cooker. Stir in salsa and beef seasoning.

- Cover and cook on HIGH for 4 to 5 hours.

- When ready to serve, sprinkle cheese over hash. Serves 8.

All-the-Trimmins Corned Beef

1 (4 - 5 pound) corned
  beef brisket   2 - 2.5 kg
4 large potatoes,
  peeled, quartered
6 carrots, peeled, halved
4 onions
1 head cabbage

- Place corned beef in roasting pan, cover with water and bring to a boil. Turn heat down and simmer for 3 hours. (Add water if necessary.)

- Add potatoes, carrots and onions. Cut cabbage into eighths and lay over top of other vegetables.

- Bring to a boil, turn heat down and cook for additional 30 to 40 minutes until vegetables are done. When slightly cool, slice corned beef across grain. Serves 8 to 10.

Beef Patties with Mushroom Gravy

1 pound lean
    ground beef   455 g
¼ cup chili sauce   70 g
1 egg, beaten
¾ cup crushed
    corn flakes   20 g
Canola oil
2 (10 ounce) cans
    cream of
    mushroom soup   2 (280 g)

- Combine ground beef, chili sauce, egg, corn flakes and a little salt and pepper in bowl and mix well. Shape into 4 patties, about ¾-inch (1.8 cm) thick.

- Place patties in skillet with a little oil, brown each patty on high heat.

- Reduce heat, cover and simmer for 10 to 15 minutes.

- Combine soups with ½ cup (125 ml) water in bowl and mix well.

- Spoon mixture over patties and simmer for about 10 minutes. Serves 4.

TIP: This gravy is great served over mashed potatoes or hot biscuits.

When purchasing ground beef, remember that fat greatly contributes to its flavor. The lower the fat content, the drier it will be once cooked.

Taco Bueno Bake

2 pounds ground beef 910 g
1½ cups taco sauce 410 g
2 (15 ounce) cans
  Spanish rice 2 (425 g)
1 (8 ounce) package
  shredded Mexican
  4-cheese blend,
  divided 230 g

- Preheat oven to 350° (175° C).

- Brown ground beef in skillet and drain. Add taco sauce, rice and half cheese. Spoon mixture into sprayed 3-quart (3 L) baking dish.

- Cover and bake for 35 minutes. Uncover and sprinkle remaining cheese on top and return to oven for 5 minutes. Serves 8.

Simple Casserole Supper

1 pound lean ground beef 455 g
¼ cup white rice 25 g
1 (10 ounce) can French
  onion soup 280 g
1 (6 ounce) can
  french-fried onion
  rings 170 g

- Preheat oven to 325° (160° C).

- Brown ground beef, drain and place in sprayed 7 x 11-inch (18 x 28 cm) baking dish. Add rice, onion soup and ½ cup (125 ml) water.

- Cover and bake for 40 minutes. Uncover, sprinkle onion rings over top and return to oven for 10 minutes. Serves 6.

Skillet Beef and Pasta

1 (8 ounce) package spiral pasta	170 g
1 (14 ounce) can beef broth	400 g
1 pound lean ground beef	455 g
2 (11 ounce) cans Mexicorn®, drained	2 (310 g)
1 (12 ounce) package cubed Mexican Velveeta® cheese	340 g

- Cook pasta according to package directions, except for water. Instead of 6 cups (1.4 L) water in directions, use 4¼ (1.1 L) cups water and beef broth.

- While pasta cooks, brown beef in large skillet, stir and drain.

- Stir in corn and cheese and cook on low heat until cheese melts.

- Gently stir cooked pasta into beef mixture until it coats pasta.

- Spoon mixture into serving bowl and garnish with few springs parsley, if desired. Serves 8.

---

*Stock or broth is a strained, thin, clear liquid in which
meat, poultry or fish simmers with vegetables and herbs.
Make your own or shop for reduced sodium, low-fat canned broth.*

Slow-Cook Beef Noodles

1½ pounds lean
  ground beef   680 g
1 (16 ounce) package
  frozen onions
  and bell peppers,
  thawed   455 g
1 (16 ounce) box
  cubed Velveeta®
  cheese   455 g
2 (15 ounce) cans
  Mexican stewed
  tomatoes, with
  liquid   2 (425 g)
2 (15 ounce) cans
  whole kernel corn,
  drained   2 (425 g)
1 (8 ounce) package
  medium egg
  noodles   230 g
1 cup shredded
  cheddar cheese   115 g

- Brown ground beef in skillet and drain fat. Place beef in 5 to 6-quart (5 to 6 L) slow cooker, add onions and bell peppers, cheese, tomatoes, corn and about ½ teaspoon (2 ml) salt and mix well. Cover and cook on LOW for 4 to 5 hours.

- Cook noodles according to package direction, drain and fold into beef-tomato mixture.

- Cook for additional 30 minutes to heat thoroughly.

- When ready to serve, top with cheddar cheese, several sprinkles of chopped fresh parsley or chopped fresh green onions, if you like. Serves 8.

Tex-Mex Supper

1 pound lean ground beef 455 g
1 large onion, chopped
1 (15 ounce) can pinto
    beans, drained   425 g
1½ teaspoons cumin   7 ml
½ head lettuce, torn
2 tomatoes, chopped
1 avocado, diced
3 green onions, chopped
1 (8 ounce) package
    shredded cheddar
    cheese   230 g
1 (10 ounce) bag corn
    chips, slightly crushed 280 g
1 (8 ounce) bottle
    Catalina salad
    dressing   230 g

- Saute beef and onion in skillet. Drain grease and add beans, cumin and 1 cup (250 ml) water and simmer until water is absorbed.

- Combine lettuce, tomatoes, avocado and onions in large bowl.

- When ready to serve, add warm beef mixture, cheese, chips, three-fourths dressing, add more if need and toss. Serve immediately. Serves 8.

Oriental Beef and Noodles

1¼ pounds
  ground beef   570 g
2 (3 ounce) packages
  Oriental-flavored
  ramen noodles   2 (85 g)
1 (16 ounce) package
  frozen Oriental
  stir-fry mixture   455 g
½ teaspoon ground
  ginger   2 ml
3 tablespoons thinly
  sliced green
  onions   20 g

- Brown ground beef in large skillet and drain.

- Add ½ cup (125 ml) water and a little salt and pepper to beef in skillet, simmer for 10 minutes and transfer to separate bowl.

- In same skillet, combine 2 cups (500 ml) water, noodles (broken up), vegetables, ginger and both seasoning packets.

- Bring to boil and reduce heat.

- Cover and simmer for 3 minutes or until noodles are tender and stir once.

- Return beef to skillet and stir in green onions. Serve right from skillet. Serves 8.

Two ounces dry pasta will make about 1 cup cooked pasta. Spaghetti and macaroni products usually double in volume when cooked. Egg noodles don't expand quite as much.

Easy Meat 'n Potatoes

1 pound ground beef	455 g
1 (10 ounce) can sloppy Joe sauce	280 g
1 (10 ounce) can fiesta nacho cheese soup	280 g
1 (32 ounce) package frozen hash-brown potatoes, thawed	910 g

- Preheat oven to 400° (205° C).

- Brown beef in skillet over medium heat and drain. Add sloppy Joe sauce and fiesta nacho cheese soup to beef and mix well.

- Place hash browns in sprayed 9 x 13-inch (23 x 33 cm) baking dish and top with beef mixture. Cover and bake for 25 minutes. Uncover and bake for additional 10 minutes. Serves 6.

TIP: This is really good sprinkled with 1 cup (115 g) shredded cheddar cheese.

Chili Casserole

1 (40 ounce) can chili with beans	1.1 kg
1 (4 ounce) can chopped green chilies	115 g
1 (2 ounce) can sliced ripe olives, drained	60 g
1 (8 ounce) package shredded cheddar cheese	230 g
2 cups ranch-flavored tortilla chips, crushed	120 g

- Preheat oven to 350° (175° C).

- Combine all ingredients in bowl and transfer to sprayed 3-quart (3 L) baking dish.

- Bake for 35 minutes or until it bubbles. Serves 8.

Cowboy's Tin Plate Supper

1½ pounds lean ground
  beef   680 g
2 onions, coarsely
  chopped
5 medium potatoes,
  peeled, sliced
1 (15 ounce) can kidney
  beans, rinsed, drained   425 g
1 (15 ounce) can pinto
  beans, drained   425 g
1 (15 ounce) can Mexican
  stewed tomatoes   425 g
1 (10 ounce) can tomato
  soup   280 g
½ teaspoon basil   2 ml
½ teaspoon oregano   2 ml
2 teaspoons minced garlic 10 ml

- Sprinkle beef with a little salt and pepper in skillet, brown meat and drain.

- Place onions in slow cooker and spoon beef over onions.

- On top of beef, layer potatoes, kidney beans and pinto beans.

- Pour stewed tomatoes and tomato soup over beans and potatoes.

- Sprinkle with basil, oregano and garlic.

- Cover and cook on LOW for 7 to 8 hours. Serves 8 to 10.

The round white potato and the round red potato are both best suited for boiling. The round white potato has a speckled brown skin and the round red has a red skin. Both have less starch than baking potatoes and more moisture. They are well suited to boiling and are used for mashed potatoes.

Ravioli and More

1 pound lean ground beef	455 g
1 teaspoon garlic powder	5 ml
1 large onion, chopped	
2 grated zucchini squash	
¼ cup (¼ stick) butter	60 g
1 (26 ounce) jar spaghetti sauce	740 g
1 (20 ounce) package ravioli with portobello mushrooms, cooked	570 g
1 (12 ounce) package shredded mozzarella cheese	340 g

- Preheat oven to 350° (175° C).

- Brown ground beef in large skillet until no longer pink and drain. Add garlic powder and ½ teaspoon (2 ml) each of salt and pepper.

- Cook onion and zucchini with butter in saucepan just until tender-crisp and stir in spaghetti sauce. Spread ½ cup (135 g) sauce in sprayed 9 x 13-inch (23 x 33 cm) baking dish.

- Layer half ravioli, half spaghetti sauce, half beef and half cheese. Repeat layers, but save remaining cheese for topping.

- Cover and bake for 35 minutes. Uncover and sprinkle remaining cheese on top. Let stand for 10 minutes before serving. Serves 8.

Cheesy Stuffed Bell Peppers

Stuffed peppers have to be a "down-home" special supper! In just about every casserole we make, we use bell peppers, but with this recipe you get the whole pepper with just the right "stuff" to make it delicious.

6 green bell peppers
1½ pounds lean
ground beef   680 g
½ cup chopped onion
¾ cup cooked rice   125 g
1 egg
2 (15 ounce) cans
Italian stewed
tomatoes, divided   2 (425 g)
½ teaspoon garlic
powder   2 ml
1 tablespoon
Worcestershire
sauce   15 ml
1 (8 ounce) package
shredded cheddar
cheese, divided   230 g

- Preheat oven to 350° (175° C).

- Cut off small portion of tops of bell pepper and remove seeds and membranes. Place in roasting pan with salted water and boil. Cook for 10 minutes so they will be only partially done. Drain and set aside to cool.

- Brown ground beef and onion in skillet and drain. Add rice, egg, 1 can tomatoes, garlic powder, Worcestershire sauce and about ½ teaspoon (2 ml) each of salt and pepper. Simmer for 5 minutes. Remove from heat and add 1 cup (114 g) cheese and mix well.

- Stuff peppers with meat mixture and set upright in sprayed, round baking dish. (You may have to trim little slivers off bottoms of peppers so they will sit upright.) Pour remaining can of tomatoes over top and around peppers.

- Bake for 25 minutes. Remove from oven, sprinkle remaining cheese on top and return to oven for 10 minutes until cheese melts. Serves 6.

Super Spaghetti Pie

This is a great recipe to make ahead of time and have ready for a late supper after the game or a midnight supper when teenagers demand "food"! And, it even resembles pizza.

1 (8 ounce) package
   spaghetti   230 g
⅓ cup grated parmesan
   cheese   35 g
1 egg, beaten
1 tablespoon butter,
   melted   15 ml
1 cup small curd cottage
   cheese, drained   225 g
½ pound lean ground beef 230 g
½ pound sausage   230 g
½ cup chopped onion   80 g
1 (15 ounce) can tomato
   sauce   425 g
1 teaspoon garlic powder 5 ml
1 teaspoon oregano   5 ml
½ cup shredded
   mozzarella cheese   60 g

- Preheat oven to 350° (175° C).

- Cook spaghetti according to package directions. While spaghetti is still warm, stir in parmesan cheese, egg and butter in large bowl.

- Pour into sprayed 10-inch (25 cm) pie pan and pat mixture up and around sides with spoon to form a crust. Pour cottage cheese over spaghetti crust.

- Brown ground meat, sausage and onion in skillet. Drain off fat and add tomato sauce, garlic powder, oregano and ½ teaspoon (2 ml) each of salt and pepper. Simmer for 10 minutes and stir occasionally.

- Pour meat mixture over cottage cheese. Bake for 30 minutes. Arrange mozzarella on top and return to oven until cheese melts. Serves 8.

Company Beef and Pasta

2 pounds lean, ground
    beef   910 g
2 onions, chopped
1 green bell pepper,
    chopped
¾ teaspoon garlic powder 4 ml
1 (14 ounce) jar spaghetti
    sauce   400 g
1 (15 ounce) can Italian
    stewed tomatoes   425 g
1 (4 ounce) can sliced
    mushrooms, drained 115 g
1 (8 ounce) package
    rotini pasta, divided 230 g
1½ pints sour cream,
    divided   680 g
1 (8 ounce) package sliced
    provolone cheese   230 g
1 (8 ounce) package
    shredded mozzarella
    cheese   230 g

- Preheat oven to 325° (160° C).

- Brown and cook beef in deep skillet and stir often to break up pieces. Drain off excess fat.

- Add onions, bell pepper, garlic powder, spaghetti sauce, stewed tomatoes and mushrooms and mix well. Simmer for 20 minutes.

- Cook rotini according to package directions and drain. Pour half rotini into sprayed 11 x 14-inch (30 x 36 cm) baking dish.

- Cover with half meat-tomato mixture and half sour cream. Top with half provolone cheese. Repeat process once more.

- Cover and bake for 35 minutes.

- Remove cover and sprinkle mozzarella cheese and continue baking for additional 5 minutes or until cheese melts. Serves 10.

Spaghetti Bake, etc.

1 (8 ounce) package spaghetti	230 g
1 pound lean ground beef	455 g
1 green bell pepper, finely chopped	
1 onion, chopped	
1 (10 ounce) can tomato bisque soup	280 g
1 (15 ounce) can tomato sauce	425 g
⅓ cup water	80 ml
½ teaspoon salt	2 ml
2 teaspoons Italian seasoning	10 ml
1 (8 ounce) can whole kernel corn, drained	230 g
1 (4 ounce) can black sliced olives, drained	115 g
1 (12 ounce) package shredded cheddar cheese	340 g

- Cook spaghetti according to package directions, drain and set aside. Cook beef, bell pepper and onion in skillet and drain.

- Add remaining ingredients plus ⅓ cup (75 ml) water, ½ teaspoon (2 ml) salt and spaghetti to beef mixture and stir well. Pour into sprayed 9 x 13-inch (23 x 33 cm) baking dish and cover.

- Refrigerate for 2 to 3 hours

- When ready to bake, preheat oven to 350° (175° C). Cover and bake for 45 minutes. Serves 8.

Enchilada Lasagna

1½ pounds lean
    ground beef   680 g
1 onion, chopped
1 teaspoon minced
    garlic   5 ml
1 (15 ounce) can
    enchilada sauce   425 g
1 (15 ounce) can
    stewed tomatoes   425 g
1 teaspoon cumin   5 ml
1 egg
1½ cups small curd
    cottage cheese   340 g
1 (12 ounce) package
    shredded 4-cheese
    blend, divided   340 g
8 (8 inch) corn
    tortillas, torn   8 (20 cm)
1 cup shredded
    cheddar cheese   115 g

- Preheat oven to 325° (160° C).

- Cook beef, onion and garlic in large skillet until meat is no longer pink. Stir in enchilada sauce, tomatoes, cumin and ½ teaspoon (2 ml) salt. Bring mixture to a boil, reduce heat and simmer for 20 minutes.

- Combine egg and cottage cheese in small bowl. Spread one-third of meat sauce into sprayed 9 x 13-inch (23 x 33 cm) baking dish. Top with half 4-cheese blend, tortillas and cottage cheese mixture. Repeat layers.

- Top with remaining meat sauce and sprinkle with remaining cheddar cheese. Cover and bake for 25 minutes. Uncover and bake for additional 10 minutes. Serves 8.

Taco Pie

1 pound lean ground beef 455 g
½ bell pepper, chopped
2 jalapeno peppers,
    seeded, chopped
Canola oil
1 (15 ounce) can Mexican
    stewed tomatoes   425 g
1 tablespoon chili powder 15 ml
1 (8 ounce) package
    shredded sharp
    cheddar cheese   230 g
1 (6 ounce) package
    corn muffin mix   170 g
1 egg
⅓ cup milk   75 ml

- Preheat oven to 375° (190° C).

- Brown ground beef, bell pepper and jalapeno peppers in a little oil in large skillet and drain well. Add ½ teaspoon (2 ml) salt, tomatoes, 1 cup (250 ml) water and chili powder. Cook on medium heat for about 10 minutes or until most liquid cooks out, but not dry.

- Pour into sprayed 9 x 13 inch (23 x 33 cm) glass baking dish. Sprinkle cheese on top.

- Combine corn muffin mix, egg and milk in bowl and beat well. Pour over top of cheese.

- Bake for 25 minutes or until corn muffin mix is light brown.

- Remove from oven and set aside for about 10 minutes before serving. Serves 8.

TIP: If you want to make a day ahead, put everything together except corn muffin mixture. Mix corn muffin mix just before you are ready to bake the Taco Pie.

Supper's Ready

1 pound lean ground beef 455 g
1 onion, chopped
4 tablespoons steak sauce 70 g
1 tablespoon flour   15 ml
1 (15 ounce) can baked
    beans with liquid   425 g
1 (8 ounce) can whole
    kernel corn, drained   230 g
1½ cups garlic-flavored
    croutons, crushed   60 g

- Preheat oven to 325° (160° C).

- Brown beef and onion in large skillet and drain. Stir in remaining ingredients except croutons.

- Pour into sprayed 9 x 13 inch (23 x 33 cm) baking dish. Sprinkle crouton crumbs on top.

- Bake for 45 minutes or until bubbly around edges. Serves 8.

TIP: You can make this ahead of time and freeze. When you need it, just thaw and cook.

Spiced Beef

1 pound lean ground beef 455 g
1 (1 ounce) packet taco
    seasoning mix   30 g
1 (15 ounce) can Mexican
    stewed tomatoes with
    liquid   425 g
1 (16 ounce) can kidney
    beans with liquid   455 g
1 (1 pound) package egg
    noodles   455 g

- Cook beef in skillet and drain. Add taco seasoning and ½ cup (125 ml) water and simmer for 15 minutes.

- Add stewed tomatoes and kidney beans. (You may need to add ¼ teaspoon/1 ml salt.)

- Cook egg noodles according to package directions and serve beef over noodles. Serves 6.

Super-Duper Supper

2 pounds lean ground
   beef   910 g
1 onion, chopped
1 (2 pound) package
   frozen tater tots   910 g
1 (8 ounce) package
   shredded cheddar
   cheese   230 g
2 (10 ounce) cans
   cream of
   mushroom soup   2 (280 g)
1 soup can milk

- Preheat oven to 350° (175° C).

- Crumble ground beef into sprayed 9 x 13 inch (23 x 33 cm) glass baking dish. Sprinkle with a little salt and pepper.

- Cover with onion. Top with tater tots and sprinkle cheese.

- Combine soups and milk in saucepan. Heat and stir just enough to mix in milk. Pour over casserole.

- Bake covered for 1 hour. Uncover and bake for additional 15 minutes. Serves 8.

Large scooped-out vegetables, round loaves of bread hollowed out or foil-lined flowerpots make good servers for dips.

Chili Relleno Casserole

1 pound lean ground beef	455 g
1 bell pepper, chopped	
1 onion, chopped	
1 (4 ounce) can chopped green chilies	115 g
1 teaspoon oregano	5 ml
1 teaspoon dried cilantro leaves	5 ml
¾ teaspoon garlic powder	4 ml
2 (4 ounce) cans whole green chilies	2 (115 g)
1½ cups shredded Montcrey Jack cheese	170 g
1½ cups shredded sharp cheddar cheese	170 g
3 large eggs	
1 tablespoon flour	15 ml
1 cup half-and-half cream	310 g

- Preheat oven to 350° (175° C).

- Cook meat with bell pepper and onion in skillet. Add chopped green chilies, oregano, cilantro, garlic powder and about ½ teaspoon (2 ml) each of salt and pepper.

- Seed whole chilies and spread into sprayed 9 x 13-inch (23 x 33 cm) baking dish. Cover with meat mixture and sprinkle with cheeses.

- Combine eggs and flour in bowl and beat with fork until fluffy. Add half-and-half cream, mix and pour slowly over top of meat in casserole. Bake for 35 minutes or until it is light brown. Serves 8.

Cabbage Rolls Along

This is a wonderful family recipe and a super way to get the kids to eat cabbage. Everyone who has ever had a garden has probably made some version of these well-loved cabbage rolls.

1 large head cabbage,
   cored
1½ pounds lean
   ground beef   680 g
1 egg, beaten
3 tablespoons ketchup 45 g
⅓ cup seasoned
   breadcrumbs   40 g
2 tablespoons dried
   minced onion flakes
   30 ml
2 (15 ounce) cans
   Italian stewed
   tomatoes   2 (425 g)
¼ cup cornstarch   30 g
3 tablespoons brown
   sugar   45 g
2 tablespoons
   Worcestershire
   sauce   30 ml

- Preheat oven to 325° (160° C).

- Place head of cabbage in large soup pot of boiling water for 10 minutes or until outer leaves are tender. Drain well. Rinse in cold water and remove 10 large outer leaves*. Set aside.

- Slice or shred remaining cabbage. Place into sprayed 9 x 13-inch (23 x 33 cm) baking dish.

- Combine ground beef, egg, ketchup, breadcrumbs, onion flakes and 1 teaspoon (5 ml) salt in large bowl and mix well.

- Pack together about ½ cup (70 g) meat mixture and put on each cabbage leaf. Fold in sides and roll leaf to completely enclose filling. (You may have to remove thick vein from cabbage leaves for easier rolling.) Place each rolled leaf over shredded cabbage.

continued next page...

- Place stewed tomatoes in large saucepan. Combine cornstarch, brown sugar and Worcestershire sauce in bowl and spoon mixture into tomatoes. Cook on high heat, stirring constantly until stewed tomatoes and juices thicken. Pour over cabbage rolls. Cover and bake for 1 hour. Serves 10.

TIP: To get that many large leaves, you may have to put 2 smaller leaves together to make one roll.

Shepherds' Pie

1 pound lean ground beef	455 g
1 (1 ounce) packet taco seasoning mix	30 g
1 cup shredded cheddar cheese	240 ml
1 (8 ounce) can whole kernel corn, drained	230 g
2 cups cooked instant mashed potatoes	420 g

- Preheat oven to 350° (175° C).

- Brown beef in skillet, cook for 10 minutes and drain. Add taco seasoning and ¾ cup (175 ml) water and cook for an additional 5 minutes.

- Spoon beef mixture into 8-inch (20 cm) baking pan, sprinkle cheese on top. Sprinkle with corn and spread mashed potatoes over top. Bake for 25 minutes or until top is golden. Serves 5.

Enchilada Casserole

1½ pounds lean
   ground beef   680 g
1 package taco
   seasoning mix
Canola oil
8 flour or corn tortillas
1 cup shredded cheddar
   cheese, divided   115 g
1 onion, chopped
1 (10 ounce) can
   enchilada sauce   280 g
1 (7 ounce) can green
   chilies   200 g
1½ cups shredded
   Monterey Jack cheese 170 g
1 (8 ounce) carton sour
   cream   230 g

- Preheat oven to 350° (175° C).

- Brown beef in skillet with a little salt and pepper until it crumbles and is brown. Drain well.

- Add taco seasoning mix and 1¼ cups (310 g) water to beef and simmer for 5 minutes.

- In separate skillet pour just enough oil to cover bottom of skillet and heat until it is hot.

- Cook tortillas one at a time, until soft and limp, for about 5 to 10 seconds on each side. Drain on paper towels.

- As you cook tortillas, spoon ⅓ cup (50 g) meat mixture into center of each tortilla. Sprinkle with small amount of cheddar cheese and 1 spoonful of chopped onion. Roll and place seam-side down in sprayed 9 x 13-inch baking dish.

- After filling all tortillas, add enchilada sauce and green chilies to remaining meat mixture. Spoon over tortillas. Cover and bake for about 30 minutes.

- Uncover and sprinkle remaining cheddar cheese and Monterey Jack cheese over casserole.

- Return to oven just until cheese melts. Place dabs of sour cream over enchiladas to serve. Serves 8.

Quick Skillet

1½ pounds lean
   ground beef   680 g
⅔ cup stir-fry sauce   180 g
1 (16 ounce) package
   frozen stir-fry
   vegetables   455 g
2 (3 ounce) packages
   Oriental-flavor
   ramen noodles   2 (85 g)

- Brown and crumble ground beef in large skillet. Add 2½ cups (625 ml) water, stir-fry sauce, vegetables and seasoning packets with ramen noodles.

- Cook and stir on medium-low heat for about 5 minutes.

- Break noodles, add to beef-vegetable mixture and cook for about 6 minutes. Stir to separate noodles as they soften. Serves 8.

Potato-Beef Casserole

4 medium potatoes,
   peeled, sliced
1¼ pounds lean ground
   beef, browned,
   drained   570 g
1 (10 ounce) can cream
   of mushroom soup   280 g
1 (10 ounce) can
   vegetable beef soup   280 g

- Preheat oven to 350° (175° C).

- Combine all ingredients in large bowl. Add a little salt and pepper. Transfer to sprayed 3-quart (3 L) baking dish. Cover and bake for 1 hour 30 minutes or until potatoes are tender. Serves 4 to 6.

Pinto Bean Pie

1 pound lean ground beef	455 g
1 onion, chopped	
2 (15 ounce) cans pinto beans with liquid	2 (425 g)
1 (10 ounce) can tomatoes and green chilies with liquid	280 g
1 (3 ounce) can french-fried onion rings	85 g

- Preheat oven to 350° (175° C).

- Brown beef and onion in skillet and drain. Layer 1 can beans, beef-onion mixture and half can tomatoes and green chilies in 2-quart (2 L) baking dish and repeat layer.

- Top with onion rings and bake for 30 minutes. Serves 6.

Extra Special Queso con Carne

(Cheese with meat.)

1 pound lean ground beef	455 g
1 (16 ounce) jar medium salsa con queso	455 g
1 (16 ounce) jar salsa	455 g
1 (15 ounce) can black beans, rinsed, drained	425 g
Tortilla scoops	

- Cook meat over medium heat in skillet and stir in queso, salsa and black beans.

- Bring mixture to a boil and stir constantly. Reduce heat to low and simmer for 5 minutes.

- Serve with tortilla scoops. Serves 8.

Beef Picante Skillet

This is a good family dish!
And you can take the
skillet right to the table.

1 pound lean ground beef	455 g
1 (10 ounce) can tomato soup	280 g
1 cup chunky salsa	265 g
6 (6 inch) flour tortillas, cut into 1 inch pieces	6 (15 cm)
1¼ cups shredded cheddar cheese, divided	145 g

- Cook beef in skillet until brown and drain.

- Add soup, salsa, ¾ cup (175 ml) water, tortillas, ½ teaspoon (2 ml) salt and half cheese. Heat to a boil. Cover and cook over low heat for 5 minutes.

- Top with remaining cheese. Serve right from skillet. Serves 4 to 5.

Cheese may be frozen. Process cheeses will last 4 months frozen and cheddar or other natural cheese will keep about 6 weeks when properly wrapped. Thaw all cheese overnight in refrigerator and use soon after thawing.

Cheeseburger Supper

1 (5 ounce) box bacon and cheddar scalloped potatoes	145 g
⅓ cup milk	75 ml
¼ cup (½ stick) butter, melted	60 g
1½ pounds lean ground beef	680 g
1 onion, coarsely chopped	
Canola oil	
1 (15 ounce) can whole kernel corn with liquid	425 g
1 (8 ounce) package shredded cheddar cheese	230 g

- Place scalloped potatoes in sprayed slow cooker.

- Pour 2¼ cups (560 ml) boiling water, milk and butter over potatoes.

- Brown ground beef and onion in little oil in skillet, drain and spoon over potatoes. Top with corn.

- Cover and cook on LOW for 6 to 7 hours.

- When ready to serve, sprinkle cheese over corn. Serves 4 to 6.

Corned Beef Supper

**4 - 5 pound corned
  beef brisket   1.8 - 2.3 kg
4 large potatoes,
  peeled, quartered
6 carrots, peeled, halved
1 head cabbage**

- Place corned beef in roasting pan and cover with water. Bring to a boil. Turn heat down and simmer for 3 hours. Add water, if necessary.

- Add potatoes and carrots on and around brisket. Cut cabbage into eighths and lay over top of potatoes, carrots and brisket.

- Bring to a boil, turn heat down and cook for additional 30 to 40 minutes or until vegetables are tender. Slice corned beef across the grain. Serves 8.

*TIP: Leftover corned beef is great
  on sandwiches.*

Corned beef is beef that is cured in a salt brine, often with spice.

Corny Chili and Beans

2 (15 ounce) cans chili
   with beans   2 (425 g)
1 (15 ounce) can
   Mexican stewed
   tomatoes   425 g
1 (11 ounce) can
   Mexicorn®,
   drained   310 g
2 diced ripe avocados

- Combine chili, tomatoes and corn in microwave-safe bowl. Cover loosely and cook on HIGH in microwave for about 4 minutes.

- Stir in diced avocados and serve hot. Serves 6.

Reuben Dogs

1 (27 ounce) can
   sauerkraut, rinsed,
   drained   780 g
2 teaspoons caraway seeds 10 ml
8 all-beef wieners, halved
   lengthwise
1 cup shredded Swiss
   cheese   110 g
Thousand island salad
   dressing

- Preheat oven to 350° (175° C).

- Place sauerkraut in sprayed 2-quart (2 L) baking dish. Sprinkle caraway seeds over top and add wieners.

- Bake for 20 minutes or until they are hot. Sprinkle with cheese. Bake for additional 3 to 5 minutes or until cheese melts. Serve with salad dressing. Serves 6.

Reuben Casserole

1 (18 ounce) package
   frozen hash-brown
   potatoes, thawed   510 g
2 pounds deli corned
   beef, sliced
   ¼-inch (6 mm) thick   910 g
1 (8 ounce) bottle Russian
   salad dressing,
   divided   230 g
1 (15 ounce) can
   sauerkraut, drained   425 g
8 slices Swiss cheese

- Preheat oven to 425° (220° C).

- Place hash-brown potatoes in sprayed 9 x 13-inch (23 x 33 cm) baking dish and season with a little salt and pepper. Bake for 25 minutes.

- Place overlapping corned beef slices on top of potatoes.

- Spoon half bottle of dressing over top of beef and arrange sauerkraut over beef. Cover with slices of cheese.

- Reduce oven to 375° (190° C) and bake for 20 minutes. Serve remaining Russian dressing on the side. Serves 8.

Thaw frozen foods in the refrigerator or in the microwave, never at room temperature, which allows unsafe bacterial growth.

Quick-Friday-Night-Game Supper

2 (15 ounce) cans chili
   without beans   2 (425 g)
2 (15 ounce) cans
   pinto beans with
   juice   2 (425 g)
2 (15 ounce) cans
   beef tamales,
   unwrapped   2 (425 g)
1 (8 ounce) package
   shredded Mexican
   4-cheese blend,
   divided   230 g
Tortilla chips

- Preheat oven to 350° (175° C).
- Spoon both cans chili in sprayed 9 x 13-inch (23 x 33 cm) baking pan and spread out with back of large spoon.
- Spread beans with juice over chili. Spread tamales over beans.
- Sprinkle about ½ cup (60 g) cheese over top, cover and bake for 30 minutes.
- Remove from oven and sprinkle remaining cheese over top of casserole.
- Return to oven for just 5 minutes.
- Serve with lots of tortilla chips. Serves 8.

TIP: You might want to serve some hot thick-and-chunky salsa along with this dish.

The Central Valley of California from Sacramento to Bakersfield is, acre for acre, the richest agricultural area in the world.

Crunchy Chicken

Spicy, Tame, Light and Full of Goodness

Crunchy Chicken Contents

Tasty Chicken-Rice and Veggies

4 boneless, skinless
   chicken breast
   halves
2 (10 ounce) jars
   sweet-and-sour
   sauce   2 (280 g)
1 (16 ounce) package
   frozen broccoli,
   cauliflower and
   carrots, thawed   455 g
1 (10 ounce) package
   frozen baby peas,
   thawed   280 g
2 cups sliced celery   200 g
1 (6 ounce) package
   parmesan-butter
   rice mix   170 g
⅓ cup toasted,
   slivered almonds   55 g

- Cut chicken in 1-inch (2.5 cm) strips.

- Combine chicken, sweet-and-sour sauce and all vegetables in sprayed 6-quart (6 L) slow cooker.

- Cover and cook on LOW for 4 to 6 hours.

- When ready to serve cook parmesan-butter rice according to package directions and fold in almonds.

- Serve chicken and vegetables over parmesan-butter rice. Serves 8.

A "free-range" chicken is one that is given twice as much room as mass-produced chickens and they are free to roam indoors and outdoors. This is supposed to enhance the "chicken" flavor because they are "happy" chickens.

Golden Chicken Dinner

6 medium new potatoes with
   peels, cubed
6 medium carrots
5 boneless, skinless chicken
   breast halves
1 tablespoon dried parsley
   flakes   15 ml
1 teaspoon seasoned salt 5 ml
1 (10 ounce) can golden
   mushroom soup   280 g
1 (10 ounce) can cream
   of chicken soup   280 g
¼ cup dried mashed
   potato flakes   15 g

- Cut chicken into ½-inch (1.2 cm) pieces.

- Place potatoes and carrots in slow cooker and top with chicken breasts.

- Sprinkle parsley flakes, seasoned salt and a little pepper over chicken.

- Combine soups in bowl and spread over chicken.

- Cover and cook on LOW for 6 to 7 hours.

- Stir in potato flakes and a little water or milk if necessary to make gravy and cook for additional 30 minutes. Serves 8.

King Henry IV of France was the first to state that everyone in his realm should "have a chicken in his pot every Sunday". Later President Herbert Hoover paraphrased the saying with "a chicken in every pot".

Tortellini Supper

1 (9 ounce) package
refrigerated cheese
tortellini 250 g
1 (10 ounce) package
frozen green peas,
thawed 280 g
1 (8 ounce) carton cream
cheese with chives
and onion 230 g
½ cup sour cream 120 g
1 (9 ounce) package
frozen cooked chicken
breasts 250 g

- Cook cheese tortellini in saucepan according to package directions.

- Place peas in colander and pour hot pasta water over green peas.

- Return tortellini and peas to saucepan.

- Combine cream cheese and sour cream in smaller saucepan and heat on low, stirring well until cheese melts.

- Spoon mixture over tortellini and peas and toss with heat on low.

- Heat cooked chicken in microwave according to package directions.

- Spoon tortellini and peas in serving bowl and place chicken on top. Serves 6.

If chicken breasts cost less than 50% more per pound than whole chickens, then the breasts are a better buy.

Delightful Chicken and Veggies

4 - 5 boneless skinless, chicken breast halves
1 (15 ounce) can whole
    kernel corn, drained   425 g
1 (10 ounce) box frozen
    green peas, thawed   280 g
1 (16 ounce) jar alfredo
    sauce   455 g
1 teaspoon chicken
    seasoning   5 ml
1 teaspoon prepared
    minced garlic   5 ml
Pasta, cooked

- Brown chicken breasts in skillet and place in sprayed, oval slow cooker.

- Combine corn, peas, alfredo sauce, ¼ cup (60 ml) water, chicken seasoning and minced garlic and pour over chicken breasts. Cover and cook on LOW for 4 to 5 hours. Serve over pasta. Servers 8.

Summertime Limeade Chicken

6 large boneless, skinless chicken breast halves
1 (6 ounce) can frozen
    limeade concentrate,
    thawed   170 g
3 tablespoons brown
    sugar   35 g
½ cup chili sauce   135 g
Rice, cooked

- Sprinkle chicken breasts with a little salt and pepper and place in sprayed skillet. Cook on high heat and brown on both sides for about 10 minutes. Remove from skillet, but set aside and keep warm.

- Add limeade concentrate, brown sugar and chili sauce to skillet. Bring to a boil and cook, stirring constantly for 4 minutes.

- Return chicken to skillet and spoon sauce over chicken. Reduce heat, cover and simmer for 15 minutes. Serve over rice. Serves 6.

Chicken Supper Ready

4 - 5 carrots
6 medium new (red)
    potatoes with peels,
    quartered
4 - 5 boneless, skinless
    chicken breast halves
1 tablespoon chicken
    seasoning   15 ml
2 (10 ounce) cans
    cream of chicken
    soup   2 (280 g)
⅓ cup white wine or
    cooking wine   75 ml

- Cut carrots into ½-inch (1.2 cm) pieces.

- Place potatoes and carrots in slow cooker.

- Sprinkle chicken breasts with chicken seasoning and place over vegetables.

- Spoon soups mixed with ¼ cup (60 ml) water and wine over chicken and vegetables.

- Cover and cook on LOW for 5 to 6 hours. Serves 5.

TIP: For a tasty change, use 1 (10 ounce/280 g) can chicken soup and 1 (10 ounce/280 g) can mushroom soup instead of cream of chicken soup.

The best way to tell when chicken is done is to insert a meat thermometer into the thickest parts of the chicken near the bone. The temperature should read no lower than 160° to be safe. Another way to tell when chicken is cooked is when the juices are clear or there is no pink color next to the bone. If there is pink in the chicken it needs to cook a little longer.

Honey-Glazed Chicken

4 boneless, skinless chicken
    breast halves
Canola oil
1 (20 ounce) can pineapple
    chunks with juice   625 g
½ cup refrigerated
    dijon-style honey-
    mustard   125 g
1 green bell pepper, thinly
    sliced
1 red bell pepper, thinly
    sliced
1 (10 ounce) box couscous 280 g

- Cut chicken breasts into strips,
  add a little salt and pepper and
  brown in large skillet with a
  little oil.

- Add juice from pineapple, cover
  and simmer for 15 minutes.

- Add honey-mustard, bell pepper
  slices and pineapple chunks to
  chicken. Bring to a boil, reduce
  heat, cover and simmer for
  additional 15 minutes. Serve
  over couscous. Serves 4.

*While some consider couscous a pasta because it is
made from semolina and water, purists tend to consider
it a separate type of food. It is grain-shaped and is
sometimes mistaken for a grain. Originally from North
Africa, it is increasingly popular in the United States.*

Chicken-Orzo Florentine

**4 boneless, skinless chicken
   breast halves**
¾ cup orzo   **120 g**
**1 (8 ounce) package fresh
   mushrooms, sliced**   **230 g**
**1 (10 ounce) package
   frozen spinach,
   thawed, well drained*** **280 g**
**1 (10 ounce) can golden
   mushroom soup**   **280 g**
½ cup mayonnaise   **110 g**
1 tablespoon lemon juice **15 ml**
**1 (8 ounce) package
   shredded Monterey
   Jack cheese, divided** **230 g**
**½ cup seasoned Italian
   breadcrumbs**   **60 g**

- Preheat oven to 350° (175° C).

- Cook chicken in boiling water for about 15 minutes and reserve broth. Cut chicken in bite-size pieces and set aside. Pour broth through strainer and cook orzo in remaining broth.

- Saute mushrooms in large, sprayed skillet until tender. Remove from heat and stir in chicken, orzo, spinach, soup, mayonnaise, lemon juice and ½ teaspoon (2 ml) pepper. Fold in half cheese and mix well.

- Spoon into sprayed 9 x 13-inch (23 x 33 cm) baking dish and sprinkle with remaining cheese and breadcrumbs. Bake for 35 minutes. Serves .

*TIP: Squeeze spinach between paper towels to completely remove excess moisture.

Lemon-Almond Chicken

Asparagus, lemon juice, curry powder and almonds give a flavorful twist to an otherwise ordinary chicken dish.

2 (14.5 ounce) cans cut asparagus, well-drained	2 (410 g)
4 boneless, skinless chicken breast halves, cut into ½-inch strips	4 (1.2 cm)
½ teaspoon seasoned salt	2 ml
3 tablespoons butter	35 g
1 (10 ounce) can cream of asparagus soup	280 g
⅔ cup mayonnaise	150 g
¼ cup milk	60 ml
1 red bell pepper, cut in strips	
2 tablespoons lemon juice	30 ml
1 teaspoon curry powder	5 ml
¼ teaspoon ground ginger	1 ml
½ cup sliced almonds, toasted	95 g

- Preheat oven to 350° (175° C).

- Place asparagus in sprayed 7 x 11-inch (18 x 28 cm) baking dish and set aside. Sprinkle chicken with seasoned salt.

- Saute chicken in butter in large skillet for about 15 minutes.

- Spoon chicken strips over asparagus. Combine asparagus soup, mayonnaise, red bell pepper, lemon juice, curry powder, ginger and ¼ teaspoon (1 ml) pepper in skillet and heat just enough to mix well.

- Spoon over chicken and sprinkle almonds over top of casserole. Bake for 35 minutes. Serves 6.

Italian Chicken over Polenta

**1 pound frozen chicken
tenders, each cut in
half**   **455 g**
Canola oil
1 onion, chopped
**1 (15 ounce) can Italian
stewed tomatoes**   **425 g**
**⅔ cup pitted kalamata
olives**   **85 g**

- Season chicken with a little
  salt and pepper. Place in large
  skillet with a little oil.

- Add onion and chicken, cook
  covered over medium-high heat
  for about 8 minutes and turn
  once. Add tomatoes and olives,
  cover and cook for additional
  8 minutes or until chicken
  is done.

Polenta:

¾ cup cornmeal   **120 g**
**⅔ cup grated parmesan
cheese**   **70 g**

- For polenta, place 2½ cups
  (625 g) water in saucepan and
  bring to a boil. Stir in cornmeal
  and ½ teaspoon (2 ml) salt and
  cook, stirring occasionally until
  mixture starts to thicken.

- Stir in cheese. Spoon polenta
  onto serving plates and top with
  chicken and sauce. Serves 6.

Spicy Orange Chicken over Noodles

1 pound boneless, skinless
   chicken tenders   455 g
2 tablespoons canola oil   30 ml
2 tablespoons soy sauce   30 ml
1 (16 ounce) package
   frozen stir-fry
   vegetables, thawed   455 g
2 cups chow mein noodles 110 g

- Lightly brown chicken tenders in oil in large skillet over medium-high heat. Add soy sauce and cook for an additional 3 minutes.

- Add stir-fry vegetables and cook for about 5 minutes or until vegetables are tender-crisp.

Sauce:

⅔ cup orange marmalade   215 g
1 tablespoon canola oil   15 ml
1 tablespoon soy sauce   15 ml
1½ teaspoons lime juice   7 ml
½ teaspoon minced ginger   2 ml
½ teaspoon cayenne
   pepper   2 ml

- Combine marmalade, oil, soy sauce, lime juice, minced ginger and cayenne pepper in saucepan and mix well.

- Heat and pour over stir-fry chicken and vegetables. Mix well and serve over chow mein noodles. Serves 6.

Creamed Chicken and Vegetables

4 large boneless, skinless chicken breast halves
1 (10 ounce) can cream of chicken soup   280 g
1 (16 ounce) package frozen peas and carrots, thawed   455 g
1 (12 ounce) jar chicken gravy   340 g

- Cut chicken in thin slices.

- Pour soup and ½ cup (125 ml) water into sprayed 6-quart (6 L) slow cooker, mix and add chicken slices.

- Sprinkle a little salt and lots of pepper over chicken and soup. Cover and cook on LOW for 4 to 5 hours.

- Add peas and carrots, chicken gravy and ½ cup (125 ml) water. Increase heat to HIGH and cook for about 1 hour or until peas and carrots are tender. Serves 6.

TIP: Serve over large, refrigerated buttermilk biscuits or over thick, Texas toast.

Do not use meats that are still frozen as they may not cook thoroughly; this is not a problem with frozen vegetables.

Sunny Chicken Supper

4 boneless, skinless chicken
    breast halves
1½ teaspoons curry
    powder   7 ml
1½ cups orange juice   375 ml
1 tablespoon brown sugar 15 ml
1 cup rice   95 g
1 teaspoon mustard   5 ml

- Rub chicken breasts with curry powder and a little salt and pepper. Combine orange juice, brown sugar, rice and mustard in large skillet and mix well.

- Place chicken breasts on top of rice mixture and bring to a boil. Reduce heat, cover and simmer for 30 minutes. Remove from heat and let stand covered for about 10 minutes until all liquid absorbs into rice. Serves 4.

Roasted Chicken and Vegetables

3 pounds chicken parts   1.4 kg
1 cup lemon pepper
    marinade with lemon
    juice, divided   250 ml
1 (16 ounce) package
    frozen mixed
    vegetables, thawed 455 g
¼ cup olive oil   60 ml

- Preheat oven to 375° (190° C).

- Arrange chicken skin-side down in sprayed baking pan. Pour ⅔ cup (150 ml) marinade over chicken.

- Bake for 30 minutes. Turn chicken over and baste with remaining ⅓ cup (75 ml) marinade.

- Toss vegetables with oil and ½ teaspoon (2 ml) salt. Arrange vegetables around chicken and cover with foil. Return pan to oven and bake for additional 30 minutes. Serves 8.

Three Cheers for Chicken

This chicken casserole is a meal in itself. Just add a tossed green salad and you have a completely, delicious, satisfying meal.

8 boneless, skinless chicken
   breast halves
6 tablespoons (¾ stick)
   butter   85 g
1 cup chopped celery   100 g
1 onion, chopped
1 small bell pepper,
   chopped
1 (4 ounce) jar chopped
   pimentos, drained   115 g
1 cup rice   95 g
1 (10 ounce) can cream
   of chicken soup   280 g
1 (10 ounce) can cream
   of celery soup   280 g
2 soup cans milk
1 (8 ounce) can sliced
   water chestnuts,
   drained   230 g
1½ cups shredded
   cheddar cheese   170 g

- Preheat oven to 325° (160° C).

- Place chicken breasts in sprayed 10 x 15-inch (25 x 38 cm) baking dish and sprinkle with a little salt and pepper.

- Melt butter in large skillet and saute celery, onion and bell pepper. Add pimentos, rice, soups, milk and water chestnuts and mix well. Pour mixture over chicken breasts.

- Cover and cook for 1 hour. Uncover and cook for additional 10 minutes. Remove from oven, sprinkle cheese over top of casserole and bake for additional 5 minutes. Serves 8 to 10.

Chicken-Tortilla Dumplings

This is not exactly a casserole, but it is a one-dish dinner and these dumplings are wonderful. This recipe is actually easy. It just takes a little time to add tortilla strips, one at a time. Using tortillas are certainly a lot easier than making up biscuit dough for the dumplings!

6 large boneless, skinless chicken breasts
2 celery ribs, chopped
1 onion, chopped
2 tablespoons chicken bouillon granules   30 ml
1 (10 ounce) can cream of chicken soup   280 g
10 (8 inch) flour tortillas   10 (18 cm)

- Place chicken breasts, 10 cups (2.5 L) water, celery and onion in very large soup pot or roasting pan. Bring to a boil, reduce heat and cook for about 30 minutes or until chicken is tender. Remove chicken and set aside to cool.

- Save broth in roasting pan. You should have about 9 cups (2.1 L) broth. Add chicken bouillon and taste to make sure it is rich and tasty. If needed, add more bouillon and more water if you don't have 9 cups (2.1 L) of broth.

- When chicken is cool enough, cut into bite-size pieces and set aside. Add chicken soup to broth and bring to boil.

- Cut tortillas into 2 x 1-inch (5 x 2.5 cm) strips. Add strips, one at a time, to briskly boiling broth mixture and stir constantly. When all strips are in saucepan, pour in chicken, reduce heat to low and simmer for 5 to 10 minutes, stirring well but gently to prevent dumplings from sticking. Serves 10 to 12.

TIP: Your pot of chicken and dumplings will be very thick. Pour into very large serving bowl and serve hot.

Stir-Fry Chicken Spaghetti

1 pound boneless, skinless chicken breast halves	**455 g**
Canola oil	
1½ cups sliced mushrooms	**110 g**
1½ cups bell pepper strips	**140 g**
1 cup sweet-and-sour stir-fry sauce	**270 g**
1 (16 ounce) package spaghetti, cooked	**455 g**
¼ cup (½ stick) butter	**30 g**

- Season chicken with a little salt and pepper and cut into thin slices. Brown chicken slices in large skillet with a little oil and cook for 5 minutes on medium-low heat. Transfer to plate and set aside.

- In same skillet with a little more oil, stir-fry mushrooms and bell pepper strips for 5 minutes. Add chicken strips and sweet-and-sour sauce and stir until ingredients are hot.

- While spaghetti is still hot, drain well, add butter and stir until butter melts. Place in large bowl and toss with chicken mixture. Serve hot. Serves 8.

Stir-Fry Cashew Chicken

Canola oil
1 pound chicken tenders,
   cut into strips   455 g
1 (16 ounce) package
   frozen broccoli,
   cauliflower and
   carrots   455 g
1 (8 ounce) jar stir-fry
   sauce   230 g
⅓ cup cashew halves   45 g
1 (12 ounce) package
   chow mein noodles 340 g

- Place a little oil and stir-fry chicken strips in 12-inch (32 cm) wok over high heat for about 4 minutes.

- Add vegetables and stir-fry an additional 4 minutes or until vegetables are tender. Stir in stir-fry sauce and cashews and cook just until mixture is hot. Serve over chow mein noodles. Serves 6.

Skillet Chicken and Peas

Canola oil
4 - 5 boneless, skinless
   chicken breast halves
2 (10 ounce) can
   cream of chicken
   soup   2 (280 g)
Paprika
2 cups instant rice   190 g
1 (10 ounce) package
   frozen green peas 280 g

- Heat a little oil in very large skillet. Add chicken and cook until it browns well. Transfer chicken to plate and keep warm.

- To same skillet, add soup, 1¾ cups (425 g) water and about ½ teaspoon (2 ml) pepper and paprika, if you have it. Heat to boiling, stir in rice and peas and reduce heat. Place chicken on top. Cover and cook on low heat for 15 minutes. Serves 6.

Skillet Chicken and More

4 boneless, skinless
   chicken breast halves
Canola oil
2 (10 ounce) cans
   cream of chicken
   soup   2 (280 g)
2 cups instant white
   rice   190 g
1 (16 ounce) package
   broccoli florets   455 g

- Brown chicken breasts on both sides in very large skillet with a little oil and simmer for 10 minutes.

- Remove chicken and keep warm. Add soup and 2 cups (500 ml) water. Heat to boiling.

- Stir in rice and broccoli florets.

- Use a little salt, pepper and paprika (if you have it) on chicken and place on top of rice.

- Cover and cook on low for 15 minutes or until liquid evaporates. Serves 8.

TIP: If you have an electric skillet, it would work great for this dish.

Bone chicken breasts with kitchen shears for a neater job.

Sassy Chicken over Tex-Mex Corn

2 teaspoons garlic powder	10 ml
1 teaspoon ground cumin	5 ml
⅔ cup flour	90 g
4 boneless, skinless chicken breast halves	
Canola oil	

- Combine garlic powder, cumin, flour and ample salt in shallow bowl. Dip chicken in flour mixture and coat each side of chicken.

- Place a little oil in heavy skillet over medium-high heat. Cut each chicken breast in half lengthwise. Brown each piece of chicken on both sides, reduce heat and add 2 tablespoons (30 ml) water to skillet.

- Cover and simmer for 15 minutes. Transfer chicken to foil-lined baking pan and place in oven at 250° (120° C) until Tex-Mex Corn is ready to serve.

Tex-Mex Corn:

1 (10 ounce) can chicken broth	280 g
1½ cups hot salsa	395 g
1 (11 ounce) can Mexicorn®	310 g
1 cup instant rice	95 g

- Use same skillet, combine broth, salsa and corn and cook for about 10 minutes.

- Stir in rice and let stand for 10 minutes or until rice is tender.

- To serve, spoon Tex-Mex Corn on platter and place chicken breasts over corn. Serves 4.

Chicken Bake Baby

1 (1 ounce) packet
    vegetable
    soup-dip mix   30 g
1 (6 ounce) package
    chicken stuffing mix   170 g
4 boneless, skinless
    chicken breast halves
1 (10 ounce) can cream
    of mushroom soup   280 g
⅓ cup sour cream   80 g

- Preheat oven to 375° (190° C).

- Toss contents of vegetable-seasoning packet, stuffing mix and 1⅔ cups (400 g) water and set aside. Place chicken in sprayed 9 x 13-inch (23 x 33 cm) baking dish.

- Mix soup and sour cream in saucepan over low heat just enough to pour over chicken. Spoon stuffing evenly over top. Bake for 40 minutes. Serves 4.

Chicken Super Supper

5 boneless, skinless chicken
    breast halves
5 slices onion
5 potatoes, peeled,
    quartered
1 (10 ounce) can cream
    of celery soup   280 g

- Preheat oven to 325° (160° C).

- Place chicken breasts in sprayed 9 x 13-inch (23 x 33 cm) baking dish. Top chicken with onion slices and place potatoes around chicken.

- Heat soup with ¼ cup (60 ml) water in saucepan just enough to pour soup over chicken and vegetables. Cover and bake for 1 hour 10 minutes. Serves 5.

Chicken Cacciatore

Chicken:

1 (2½ pound) frying
    chicken   1.1 kg
Canola oil
2 onions, sliced

- Quarter chicken and sprinkle
  with plenty of salt and pepper.
  Place in large skillet on
  medium-high heat with a little
  oil. Add sliced onions and cook
  until chicken is tender for about
  15 minutes.

Sauce:

1 (15 ounce) can stewed
    tomatoes   425 g
1 (8 ounce) can tomato
    sauce   230 g
1 teaspoon dried oregano   5 ml
1 teaspoon celery seed   5 ml

- Combine stewed tomatoes,
  tomato sauce, oregano and
  celery seed in saucepan. Bring
  mixture to a boil, reduce heat
  and simmer for about
  20 minutes. Serves 4.

*TIP: This is great over hot, cooked
    noodles or spaghetti.*

*It's no secret that tomatoes are a critical part of our cooking.
They are healthy and can be turned into many wonderful
sauces. There are many styles to choose from including
whole, crushed, stewed, diced and sun-dried. We recommend
that you keep your shelves well stocked with plenty of
canned tomatoes because many recipes include them.*

Chicken and the Works

6 boneless, skinless
  chicken breast halves
Paprika
Canola oil
2 (10 ounce) cans
  cream of chicken
  soup   2 (280)
2 cups instant rice   190 g
1 (10 ounce) package
  frozen green peas,
  thawed   280 g

- Sprinkle chicken with pepper
  and paprika and brown in
  large, 12-inch (32 cm) skillet
  with a little oil. Reduce heat,
  cover and simmer for about
  15 minutes. Transfer chicken
  to plate and keep warm.

- Add soup, 2 cups (500 ml) water
  to skillet and mix well. Heat to
  boiling and stir in rice and green
  peas. Top with chicken breasts,
  cover and simmer over low heat
  for about 15 minutes. Serves 6.

Cheesy Swiss Chicken

4 boneless, skinless chicken
  breast halves
Canola oil
⅓ cup refrigerated honey-
  mustard dressing   80 ml
1 (8 slices) package fully
  cooked bacon
4 slices Swiss cheese

- Cook chicken breasts in large
  skillet with a little oil on
  medium-high heat for 5 minutes.

- Remove chicken to cutting
  board and liberally spread
  each breast with honey-
  mustard dressing.

- Top with 2 slices bacon for each
  breast and cover with 1 slice of
  Swiss cheese.

- Carefully lift each chicken
  breast back into skillet and
  place 1 tablespoon (15 ml)
  water in skillet. Cover and
  cook on medium-low heat for
  10 minutes. Serves 4.

Chicken and Sauerkraut

6 large, boneless, skinless
   chicken breast halves
1 (15 ounce) can sliced
   potatoes, drained   425 g
1 (16 ounce) can
   sauerkraut,
   drained   455 g
¼ cup pine nuts or
   ½ teaspoon
   caraway seeds   32 g/2 ml

- Season chicken in large skillet with a little pepper and cook over medium heat for 15 minutes or until chicken browns on both sides.

- Add potatoes to skillet and spoon sauerkraut over potatoes. Cover and cook over low heat for 35 minutes or until chicken is done.

- Toast pine nuts in dry skillet on medium heat until golden brown. Stir constantly. Sprinkle chicken and sauerkraut with toasted pine nuts or caraway seeds and serve. Serves 6.

TIP: This is good served with sour cream.

Broccoli-Cheese Chicken

1 tablespoon butter	15 ml
4 boneless, skinless chicken breast halves	
1 (10 ounce) can broccoli-cheese soup	280 g
1 (10 ounce) package frozen broccoli spears	280 g
⅓ cup milk	75 ml
Rice, cooked	

- Heat butter in skillet, cook chicken for 15 minutes or until brown on both sides, remove and set aside.

- In same skillet, combine soup, broccoli, milk and a little pepper and heat to boiling, return chicken to skillet and reduce heat to low.

- Cover and cook for additional 25 minutes until chicken is no longer pink and broccoli is tender. Serve over rice. Serves 4.

Rice came to the South when a storm-ravaged merchant ship sailing from Madagascar reached the port of Charleston for safe haven. As a gift to the people, the ship's captain gave a local planter "Golden Seed Rice" and by 1700, rice was a major crop in the colonies. The success of the crop gave rise to the name "Carolina Gold Rice'.

Alfredo Chicken

5 - 6 boneless, skinless
   chicken breast halves
Canola oil
1 (16 ounce) package
   frozen broccoli florets,
   thawed   455 g
1 red bell pepper, seeded,
   chopped
1 (16 ounce) jar alfredo
   sauce   455 g

- Preheat oven to 325° (160° C).

- Brown and cook chicken breasts
  in large skillet with a little
  oil until juices run clear.

- Transfer to sprayed 9 x 13-inch
  (23 x 33 cm) baking dish.

- Microwave broccoli according
  to package directions and drain.
  (If broccoli stems are extra long,
  trim and discard.)

- Spoon broccoli and bell pepper
  over chicken.

- Heat alfredo sauce with
  ¼ cup (60 ml) water in small
  saucepan.

- Pour over chicken and
  vegetables. Cover and cook for
  15 to 20 minutes. Serves 6.

TIP: *This chicken-broccoli dish
can be "dressed up" a bit by
sprinkling a little shredded
parmesan cheese over the top
after casserole comes out of
the oven.*

*Hydrogenated oil is made from the cheapest oil-producing
plants possible, usually cottonseed, corn and soybeans.
Walter Willet, principle member of the Harvard Nurses' health
study (the largest single controlled study in human history),
suggests that hydrogenated oil is the worst food we are
currently consuming. (Corn syrup is a close second.)*

Savory Chicken Fettuccini

2 pounds boneless, skinless
    chicken thighs, cubed 910 g
½ teaspoon garlic powder 2 ml
½ teaspoon black pepper 2 ml
1 red bell pepper,
    chopped
2 ribs celery, chopped
1 (10 ounce) can cream
    of celery soup   280 g
1 (10 ounce) can cream
    of chicken soup   280 g
1 (8 ounce) package
    cubed Velveeta®
    cheese   230 g
1 (4 ounce) jar diced
    pimentos   115 g
1 (16 ounce) package
    spinach fettuccini   455 g

- Place chicken in slow cooker.

- Sprinkle with garlic powder, black pepper, bell pepper and celery. Top with soups.

- Cover and cook on HIGH for 4 to 6 hours or until chicken juices are clear.

- Stir in cheese and pimentos. Cover and cook until cheese melts.

- Cook fettuccini according to package directions and drain.

- Place fettuccini in serving bowl and spoon chicken over fettuccini. Serve hot. Serves 10.

Imperial Chicken

1 (6 ounce) box long
   grain-wild rice   170 g
1 (16 ounce) jar roasted
   garlic parmesan
   cheese creation sauce 455 g
6 boneless, skinless
   chicken breast halves
1 (16 ounce) box frozen
   French-style green
   beans, thawed   455 g
½ cup slivered almonds,
   toasted   85 g

- Pour in 2½ cups (625 g) water, rice and seasoning packet in sprayed oval slow cooker and stir well.

- Spoon in cheese creation and mix well.

- Place chicken breasts in slow cooker and cover with green beans.

- Cover and cook on LOW for 3 to 5 hours.

- When ready to serve, sprinkle with slivered almonds.
Serves 6.

Each man, woman and child eats about 80 tomatoes annually in the form of fresh, processed, chopped, stewed, ketchup, sauces, juices and hundreds of consumer products that use tomatoes.

Chicken Parmesan and Spaghetti

1 (14 ounce) package
frozen, cooked,
breaded chicken
cutlets, thawed   400 g
1 (28 ounce) jar
spaghetti sauce,
divided   795 g
2 (5 ounce) packages
grated parmesan
cheese, divided   2 (145 g)
1 (8 ounce) package
thin spaghetti,
cooked   230 g

- Preheat oven to 400° (205° C).

- Place cutlets in sprayed 9 x 13-inch (23 x 33 cm) baking dish. Top each with about ¼ cup (70 g) spaghetti sauce and 1 heaping tablespoon (15 ml) parmesan. Bake for 15 minutes.

- Place cooked spaghetti on serving platter and top with cutlets. Sprinkle remaining cheese over cutlets. Heat remaining spaghetti sauce and serve with chicken and spaghetti. Serves 6 to 8.

Researchers have found that tomatoes have a large amount of lycopene in them. Lycopene has more than twice the amount of powerful antioxidents and 100 times more than vitamins E and C. The high vitamin, mineral and nutrient values of tomatoes may help slow down the aging process and some degenerative diseases such as cancers, cardio-vascular disease and blindness.

Hawaiian Chicken

2 small, whole chickens,
   quartered
Flour
Canola oil
1 (20 ounce) can sliced
   pineapple with juice   570 g
2 bell peppers, cut in strips
Rice, cooked

- Preheat oven to 350° (175° C). Wash and pat chicken dry with paper towels. Shake a little salt, pepper and flour on chicken. Brown chicken in oil and place in 10 x 15-inch (25 x 38 cm) baking pan.

- Drain pineapple into 2-cup (500 ml) measure. Add water (or orange juice if you have it) to make 1½ cups (375 ml) liquid. Reserve juice for sauce.

Sauce:

1 cup sugar	200 g
3 tablespoons cornstarch	20 g
¾ cup vinegar	175 ml
l tablespoon lemon juice	15 ml
1 tablespoon soy sauce	15 ml
2 teaspoons chicken bouillon granules	10 ml

- Combine 1½ cups (375 ml) juice, sugar, cornstarch, vinegar, lemon juice, soy sauce and chicken bouillon in medium saucepan.

- Bring to a boil, stir constantly until thick and clear and pour over chicken. Cover and bake for 40 minutes.

- Place pineapple slices and bell pepper on top of chicken and bake for additional 10 minutes. Serve over white rice. Serves 8.

Almond-Crusted Chicken

1 egg
¼ cup seasoned
    breadcrumbs   30 g
1 cup slivered almonds   170 g
4 boneless, skinless
    chicken breast halves
1 (5 ounce) package
    grated parmesan
    cheese   145 g

- Preheat oven to 350° (175° C).

- Place egg and 1 teaspoon (5 ml) water in shallow bowl and beat. In another shallow bowl, combine breadcrumbs and almonds.

- Dip each chicken breast in egg, then in almond mixture and place in sprayed 9 x 13-inch (23 x 33 cm) baking pan. Bake for 20 minutes.

- Remove chicken from oven and sprinkle parmesan cheese over each breast. Cook for additional 15 minutes or until almonds and cheese are golden brown.

Sauce:

1 teaspoon minced garlic   5 ml
⅓ cup finely chopped
    onion   55 g
2 tablespoons canola oil   30 ml
1 cup white wine   250 ml
¼ cup teriyaki sauce   60 ml

- Saute garlic and onion in saucepan with oil. Add wine and teriyaki. Bring to a boil, reduce heat and simmer for about 10 minutes or until mixture reduces by half.

- When serving, divide sauce among four plates and place chicken breast on top. Serves 4.

Chicken and Everything Good

2 (10 ounce) cans
   cream of chicken
   soup   2 (280 g)
⅓ cup (⅔ stick)
   butter, melted   75 g
3 cups cooked, cubed
   chicken   420 g
1 (16 ounce) package
   frozen broccoli,
   corn and red bell
   peppers   455 g
1 (10 ounce) package
   frozen green peas 280 g
1 (8 ounce) package
   cornbread
   stuffing mix   230 g

- Combine soup, butter and ⅓ cup (75 ml) water in bowl and mix well.
- Add chicken, vegetables and stuffing mix and stir well. Spoon mixture into sprayed large slow cooker.
- Cover and cook on LOW for 5 to 6 hours or on HIGH for 2 hours 30 minutes to 3 hours. Serves 8.

Use different coatings on chicken for a variety of flavors: cracker crumbs, unsweetened cereal, corn flakes, bran, half flour and half cornstarch, and flour and oat bran.

Hurry-Up Chicken Enchiladas

2½ -3 cups cooked,
  cubed chicken
  breast   350 - 420 g
1 (10 ounce) can
  cream of chicken
  soup   280 g
1½ cups chunky salsa,
  divided   395 g
8 (6 inch) flour
  tortillas   8 (15 cm)
1 (10 ounce) can
  fiesta nacho
  cheese soup   280 g

- Combine chicken, soup and ½ cup (130 g) salsa in saucepan and heat. Spoon about ⅓ cup (70 g) chicken mixture in center of each tortilla and roll tortilla.

- Place seam-side down in sprayed 9 x 13-inch (23 x 33 cm) baking dish. Mix nacho cheese soup, remaining salsa and ¼ cup (60 ml) water and pour over enchiladas.

- Cover with wax paper and microwave on HIGH, turning several times for 5 minutes or until bubbly. Serves 6.

When you need cooked chicken, boil it in water and turn off heat after it is three-quarters cooked. Cover the pot and leave chicken in the pot for about 1 hour to finish cooking. This method produces juicier and more tender chicken.

Catch-a-Chicken Casserole

3 cups cooked, chopped chicken or turkey	420 g
1 (16 ounce) package frozen broccoli florets, thawed	455 g
1 (10 ounce) can cream of chicken soup	280 g
⅔ cup mayonnaise	150 g
1 cup shredded cheddar cheese	115 g
1½ cups crushed cheese crackers	90 g

- Preheat oven to 350° (175° C).

- Combine chicken, broccoli, soup, mayonnaise and cheese in bowl and mix well.

- Pour into sprayed 3-quart (3 L) baking dish and spread cheese crackers over top.

- Bake for 40 minutes. Serves 6 to 8.

Family Chicken Casserole

1 (7 ounce) box chicken-flavored rice and macaroni	200 g
3 cups cooked, chopped chicken or turkey	420 g
1 (10 ounce) can cream of mushroom soup	280 g
1 (10 ounce) can cream of celery soup	280 g
1 (10 ounce) package frozen peas, thawed	280 g
1 cup shredded cheddar cheese	115 g

- Preheat oven to 350° (175° C).

- Cook rice and macaroni according to package directions.

- Combine chicken, cooked rice-macaroni mixture, soups mixed with ½ cup (125 ml) water, peas, cheese and ½ cup (125 ml) water in bowl and mix well.

- Pour into sprayed 3-quart (3 L) baking dish. Cover and bake for 40 minutes. Serves 8.

Speedy Chicken Pie

This is a "speedy" lunch that gives you extra time to create a special "outta-sight" dessert.

1 (12 ounce) package shredded cheddar cheese, divided	340 g
1 (10 ounce) package frozen, chopped broccoli, thawed, drained	280 g
2 cups cooked, finely diced chicken breasts	280 g
½ cup finely chopped onion	80 g
½ cup finely chopped red bell pepper	75 g
1⅓ cups half-and-half cream	415 g
3 eggs	
¾ cup biscuit mix	90 g

- Preheat oven to 350° (175°).

- Combine 2 cups (228 g) cheddar cheese, broccoli, chicken, onion and bell pepper in bowl.

- Spread into sprayed 10-inch (25 cm) pie pan.

- In separate bowl, beat half-and-half cream, eggs, biscuit mix, ½ teaspoon (2 ml) salt and ¼ teaspoon (1 ml) pepper and mix well.

- Slowly pour cream-egg mixture over broccoli-chicken mixture, but do not stir.

- Cover and bake for 35 minutes or until center of pie is firm.

- Uncover and sprinkle remaining cheese over top.

- Return to oven for about 5 minutes or just until cheese melts. Serves 8.

It is best to brown chicken over medium heat. High heat will make the outside stringy.

Encore Chicken

Canola oil
6 boneless, skinless chicken
   breast halves
1 (16 ounce) jar thick-and-
   chunky hot salsa   455 g
1 cup packed light brown
   sugar   220 g
1 tablespoon dijon-style
   mustard   15 ml
Brown rice, cooked

- Preheat oven to 325° (160° C).

- In large skillet with a little oil, brown chicken breasts and place in sprayed 9 x 13-inch (23 x 33 cm) baking dish.

- Combine salsa, brown sugar, mustard and ½ teaspoon (2 ml) salt in bowl and pour over chicken. Cover and bake for 45 minutes. Serve over brown rice. Serves 6.

Parmesan Chicken

1 (.04 ounce) packet
   Italian salad dressing
   mix   10 g
½ cup grated parmesan
   cheese   100 g
¼ cup flour   30 g
¾ teaspoon garlic powder 4 ml
5 boneless, skinless chicken
   breast halves

- Preheat oven to 375° (190° C).

- Combine salad dressing mix, parmesan cheese, flour and garlic in shallow bowl.

- Moisten chicken with a little water and coat with cheese mixture. Place in sprayed 9 x 13-inch (23 x 33 cm) baking pan.

- Bake for 25 minutes or until chicken is light brown and cooks thoroughly. Serves 6.

Comfort Chicken Plus

1 (6 ounce) box chicken
   stuffing mix   **170 g**
1 bunch fresh broccoli
   florets
2 ribs celery, sliced
1 cup chopped red bell
   pepper   **150 g**
2 tablespoons butter **30 g**
1 (8 ounce) can whole
   kernel corn, drained **230 g**
2½ cups finely chopped
   chicken or turkey **350 g**
1 (1 ounce) packet
   hollandaise sauce mix **30 g**
1 (3 ounce) can
   french-fried onions **85 g**

- Preheat oven to 325° (160° C).

- Prepare chicken stuffing mix according to package directions.

- Place broccoli, celery, bell pepper, butter and ¼ cup (60 ml) water in microwave-safe bowl. Cover with wax paper and microwave on HIGH for 1½ minutes.

- Add broccoli-celery mixture, corn and chicken to stuffing and mix well. Spoon into sprayed 7 x 11-inch (18 x 28 cm) baking dish.

- Prepare hollandaise sauce according to package directions, but use 1¼ cups (310 g) water instead of 1 cup (250 ml) water stated. Pour hollandaise sauce over casserole and sprinkle top with fried onions.

- Bake for 25 minutes. Serves 8.

It's best to put crunchy foods like celery in soups or stews toward the end of the cooking time so they will stay crunchy.

Tasty Skillet Chicken

5 large boneless, skinless chicken breast halves
Canola oil
1 green bell pepper, seeded, thinly sliced
1 red bell pepper, seeded, thinly sliced
2 small yellow squash, seeds removed, thinly sliced
1 (16 ounce) bottle thick-and-chunky salsa   455 g
2 (9 ounce) packages ready buttery rice, cooked   2 (250 g)

- Cut chicken breasts into thin strips. With a little oil in large skillet, saute chicken for about 5 minutes.

- Add bell peppers and squash and cook for an additional 5 minutes or until peppers are tender-crisp.

- Stir in salsa and bring to a boil. Lower heat and simmer for 10 minutes. Serve over rice. Serves 8.

TIP: It will take 90 seconds to cook Uncle Ben's® ready buttery rice. It's a snap and great for hurry-up suppers.

To make green pepper strips or slices, hold the pepper upright on a cutting surface. Slice each of the side from the pepper stem and discard stem, white membrane and seeds.

Creamy Chicken Bake

1 (8 ounce) package egg noodles	230 g
1 (16 ounce) package frozen broccoli florets, thawed	455 g
¼ cup (½ stick) butter, melted	60 g
1 (8 ounce) package shredded cheddar cheese	230 g
1 (10 ounce) can cream of chicken soup	280 g
1 cup half-and-half cream	310 g
¼ teaspoon ground mustard	1 ml
3 cups cooked, cubed chicken breasts	420 g
⅔ cup slivered almonds, toasted	110 g

- Preheat oven to 350° (175° C).

- Cook noodles according to package directions and drain. Cut some stems off broccoli and discard. Combine noodles and broccoli in large bowl.

- Add butter and cheese and stir until cheese melts. Stir in chicken soup, half-and-half cream, mustard, chicken and about ½ teaspoon (2 ml) each of salt and pepper. Spoon into sprayed 2½-quart (2.5 L) baking dish.

- Cover and bake for about 40 minutes. Remove from oven, sprinkle with slivered almonds. Serves 8.

Chicken Supreme

It is really delicious and "so-o-o-o" easy. It is a "meal in itself"!

1 onion, chopped	
1 cup sliced celery	100 g
3 tablespoons butter	35 g
4 cups cooked, diced chicken breast	560 g
1 (6 ounce) package long grain-wild rice, cooked	170 g
1 (10 ounce) can cream of celery soup	280 g
1 (10 ounce) can cream of chicken soup	280 g
1 (4 ounce) jar pimentos	115 g
2 (15 ounce) cans French-style green beans, drained	2 (425 g)
1 cup slivered almonds	170 g
1 cup mayonnaise	225 g
1 teaspoon white pepper	5 ml
2½ cups crushed potato chips	140 g

- Preheat oven to 350° (175° C).

- Saute onion and celery in butter in saucepan. In very large saucepan, combine onion-celery mixture, chicken, rice, soups, pimentos, green beans, almonds, mayonnaise, ½ teaspoon (2 ml) salt and white pepper and mix well.

- Spoon into sprayed 10 x 15-inch (25 x 38 cm) deep baking dish. Sprinkle crushed potato chips over top of casserole. Bake for 40 minutes or until potato chips are light brown. Serves 14.

TIP: This recipe is a great way to serve a lot of people. It will serve at least 14 to 15. It may also be made with green peas instead of green beans. If you want to make it in advance and freeze or just refrigerate for the next day, just wait until you are ready to cook the casserole before adding potato chips.

Divine Chicken Casserole

1 (16 ounce) package frozen broccoli spears, thawed	455 g
1 (10 ounce) box frozen broccoli spears, thawed	280 g
1 teaspoon seasoned salt	5 ml
3 cups cooked, diced chicken	420 g
1 (10 ounce) can cream of chicken soup	280 g
2 tablespoons milk	30 ml
½ cup mayonnaise	110 g
2 teaspoons lemon juice	10 ml
½ teaspoon white pepper	2 ml
1 cup shredded cheddar cheese	115 g
1½ cups round buttery cracker crumbs	90 g
3 tablespoons butter, melted	35 g

- Preheat oven to 350° (175° C).

- Cook broccoli according to package directions and drain. Cut some of the stems away and discard.

- Place broccoli spears in sprayed 9 x 13-inch (23 x 33 cm) baking dish and sprinkle seasoned salt over broccoli. Cover with diced chicken.

- Combine soup, milk, mayonnaise, lemon juice, white pepper and cheese in saucepan and heat just enough to be able to pour mixture over broccoli and chicken.

- Combine cracker crumbs and butter in bowl and sprinkle over casserole. Bake for 35 to 40 minutes or until hot and bubbly. Serves 8.

Family Night Spaghetti

6 frozen breaded, cooked
  chicken breast halves
1 (8 ounce) package
  spaghetti, cooked   230 g
1 (14 ounce) jar spaghetti
  sauce   400 g
1 (12 ounce) package
  shredded mozzarella
  cheese, divided   340 g

- Bake chicken breasts according
  to package directions and keep
  warm. Cook spaghetti according
  to package directions, drain and
  arrange on platter.

- Place spaghetti sauce in
  saucepan with 1 cup (115 g)
  mozzarella cheese and heat
  slightly, but do not boil.

- Spoon about half sauce over
  spaghetti and arrange chicken
  breast over top. Spoon
  remaining spaghetti sauce on
  chicken and sprinkle remaining
  cheese over top. Serves 6.

Skillet Chicken and Stuffing

1 (6 ounce) box stuffing
  mix for chicken with
  seasoning packet   170 g
1 (16 ounce) package
  frozen whole kernel
  corn   455 g
¼ cup (½ stick) butter   60 g
4 boneless, skinless
  chicken breast halves,
  cooked

- Combine seasoning packet,
  corn, 1⅔ cups (400 g) water and
  butter in large skillet and bring
  to a boil. Reduce heat, cover
  and simmer for 5 minutes.

- Stir in stuffing mix just until
  moist. Cut chicken into thin
  slices and mix with stuffing-corn
  mixture. Cook on low heat
  just until mixture heats well.
  Serves 6.

Easy Chicken and Dumplings

3 cups cooked,
chopped chicken   420 g
2 (10 ounce) cans
cream of chicken
soup   2 (280 g)
3 teaspoons chicken
bouillon granules   15 ml
1 (8 ounce) can
refrigerated
buttermilk
biscuits   230 g

- Combine chopped chicken, both cans of soup, chicken bouillon granules and 4½ cups (1.1 L) water in large, heavy pan. Boil mixture and stir to mix well.

- Separate biscuits and cut in half, cut again making 4 pieces out of each biscuit. Drop biscuit pieces 1 at a time, into boiling chicken mixture and stir gently.

- When all biscuits are dropped, reduce heat to low and simmer, stirring occasionally for about 15 minutes. Serves 8.

TIP: Deli turkey will work just fine in this recipe. It's a great time-saver!

Use mayonnaise (not low-fat) to get a crispy, golden brown exterior on chicken by rubbing it all over the outside before roasting.

Family Chicken Bake

This is such a good, basic "meat-and-potato" dish all families love.

¼ cup (½ stick) butter	60 g
1 red bell pepper, seeded, chopped	
1 onion, chopped	
2 ribs celery, chopped	
1 (8 ounce) carton sour cream	230 g
1½ cups half-and-half cream	470 g
1 (7 ounce) can chopped green chilies, drained	200 g
1 teaspoon chicken bouillon granules	5 ml
½ teaspoon celery salt	2 ml
3 - 4 cups cooked, cubed chicken	420 - 560 g
1 (16 ounce) package shredded cheddar cheese, divided	455 g
1 (2 pound) package frozen hash-brown potatoes, thawed	910 g

- Preheat oven to 350° (175° C).

- Melt butter in saucepan and saute bell pepper, onion and celery.

- Combine sour cream, half-and-half cream, green chilies, bouillon, celery salt and about ½ teaspoon (2 ml) each of salt and pepper in large bowl.

- Stir in bell pepper mixture, chicken and half of cheese. Fold in hash-brown potatoes. Spoon into sprayed 10 x 15-inch (25 x 38 cm) baking dish.

- Bake for 45 minutes or until casserole is bubbly. Remove from oven and sprinkle remaining cheese over top of casserole. Return to oven for about 5 minutes. Serves 10.

TIP: And for a change of pace, heat some hot, thick-and-chunky salsa to spoon over top of each serving.

Chicken Pot Pie

1 (15 ounce) package
    refrigerated piecrusts   425 g
1 (19 ounce) can cream
    of chicken soup   540 g
2 cups cooked, diced
    chicken breast   280 g
1 (10 ounce) package
    frozen mixed
    vegetables, thawed   280 g

- Preheat oven to 325° (160° C).

- Place 1 piecrust in 9-inch
  (23 cm) pie pan. Fill with
  chicken soup, chicken and
  mixed vegetables.

- Cover with second layer of
  piecrust; fold edges under and
  crimp. With knife, cut 4 slits in
  center of piecrust.

- Bake for 1 hour 15 minutes or
  until crust is golden. Serves 6.

TIP: When you're too busy to cook
    a chicken, get the rotisserie
    chickens from the grocery
    store. They are great.

Chicken-Broccoli Skillet

3 cups cooked, cubed,
    chicken   420 g
1 (16 ounce) package
    frozen broccoli florets 455 g
1 (8 ounce) package
    cubed Velveeta®
    cheese   230 g
⅔ cup mayonnaise   150 g

- Combine chicken, broccoli,
  cheese and ¼ cup (60 ml) water
  in skillet. Cover and cook over
  medium heat until broccoli is
  tender-crisp and cheese melts.
  Stir in mayonnaise and heat
  through, but do not boil.
  Serves 6.

TIP: This is great served over hot,
    cooked rice.

Chicken-Broccoli Bake

2 (3.5 ounce) bags
   rice   2 (100 g)
1 (8 ounce) package
   cubed Velveeta®
   cheese   230 g
1 (16 ounce) package
   frozen broccoli
   florets, thawed   455 g
3 cups cooked, cubed
   chicken   420 g
1 cup cracker crumbs
   or seasoned
   breadcrumbs   60 g/120 g

- Preheat oven to 325° (160° C).

- Cook rice in large sausage pan according to package directions. Stir in cheese and ¼ cup (60 ml) water. Stir and mix until cheese melts.

- Cook broccoli according to package directions. Add broccoli and chicken to rice-cheese mixture and mix well.

- Spoon into sprayed 9 x 13-inch (23 x 33 cm) baking dish. Top with cracker or seasoned breadcrumbs and bake for 15 minutes. Serves 8.

TIP: Just use deli chicken or turkey if you don't want to cook it.

Turkey Tenders with Honey-Ginger Glaze

Canola oil
Lemon pepper
1 pound turkey tenders   455 g
Rice, cooked

- Place a little oil in heavy skillet. Sprinkle lemon pepper on turkey tenders and cook for about 5 minutes on each side or until brown.

Glaze:

⅔ cup honey	230 g
2 teaspoons peeled, grated fresh ginger	10 ml
1 tablespoon marinade for chicken (Lea & Perrins)	15 ml
1 tablespoon soy sauce	15 ml
Lemon juice	

- Combine all glaze ingredients in bowl, mix well and pour into skillet with chicken tenders.

- Bring mixture to a boil, reduce heat and simmer for 15 minutes. Serve over rice. Serves 6.

TIP: You might want to try the new packages of rice that you can microwave for 90 seconds and serve.

Allow 2 to 3 days for a turkey to thaw in a refrigerator. It's best to let the thawed turkey sit at room temperature about 1 hour before cooking it.

Lemon-Honey Glazed Chicken

1 (2½ - 3 pound)
   chicken,
   quartered   1.1 - 1.4 kg
⅓ cup honey   115 g
2 tablespoons lemon juice 30 ml
1 (1 ounce) packet onion
   soup mix   30 g

- Preheat oven to375° (190° C).

- Place chicken quarters, skin-side down in sprayed 9 x 13-inch (23 x 33 cm) baking pan.

- Bake for 30 minutes. Remove from oven and turn chicken quarters over.

- Combine honey, lemon juice and onion soup mix in small bowl and brush glaze over chicken. Cook for additional 20 minutes. Brush glaze over chicken every 5 minutes. Serves 4.

Glazed Chicken and Rice

4 boneless, skinless chicken
   breast halves, cubed
1 (20 ounce) can pineapple
   chunks with juice   570 g
½ cup honey-mustard
   grill-and-glaze sauce 125 g
1 red bell pepper, seeded,
   chopped
Rice, cooked

- Brown chicken in skillet with a little oil and cook on low heat for 15 minutes.

- Add pineapple, honey-mustard and bell pepper and bring to a boil.

- Reduce heat to low and simmer for 10 to 15 minutes or until sauce thickens slightly.

- Serve over rice. Serves 4.

Skillet Roasted Chicken

1 (2½ - 3 pound)
   chicken,
   quartered   1.1 - 1.4 kg
2 teaspoons sage   10 ml
Canola oil
2 teaspoons minced
   garlic   10 ml
2 (10 ounce) cans
   cream of chicken
   soup   2 (280 g)
Rice, cooked

- Dry chicken quarters with paper towels. Sprinkle with sage and a little salt and pepper.

- Place in large skillet with a little oil. Cook on both sides over medium-high heat for about 15 minutes.

- Combine garlic, chicken soup and ½ cup (125 ml) water in saucepan. Heat just enough to blend ingredients.

- Pour over chicken, cover and cook on low heat for 5 minutes or until chicken heats thoroughly. Serve over rice. Serves 4.

Figure about ¾ cup stuffing or dressing per pound of chicken when stuffing a chicken.

Honey-Roasted Chicken

3 tablespoons soy sauce	45 ml
3 tablespoons honey	50 g
2½ cups crushed small shredded wheat cereal	80 g
½ cup very finely minced walnuts	65 g
5 - 6 boneless, skinless chicken breast halves	

- Preheat oven to 400° (205° C).

- Combine soy sauce and honey in shallow bowl and set aside. In another shallow bowl, combine crushed cereal and walnuts.

- Dip both sides of each chicken breast in soy sauce-honey mixture and dredge in cereal-walnut mixture.

- Place each piece on sprayed foil-lined baking sheet. Bake for 25 minutes (about 35 minutes if breasts are very large). Serves 6.

Italian Crumb Chicken

5 - 6 boneless, skinless chicken breast halves	
¾ cup mayonnaise	170 g
⅓ cup grated parmesan cheese	35 g
½ cup Italian-seasoned breadcrumbs	60 g

- Preheat oven to 400° (205° C).

- Place all chicken breasts on foil-lined baking pan. Combine mayonnaise, 1 teaspoon (5 ml) pepper and parmesan cheese in bowl and mix well.

- Spread mixture over chicken breasts and sprinkle seasoned breadcrumbs on both sides.

- Bake for 20 to 25 minutes or until it is light brown. Breasts may be served whole or sliced diagonally. Serves 6.

Grilled Chicken with Raspberry Barbecue Sauce

Chicken:

1 (2½ pound) chicken,
    quartered   910 g
Seasoned salt
Seasoned pepper

- Season chicken quarters liberally with seasoned salt and pepper. Grill chicken, covered with grill lid over medium-high heat for about 8 minutes on each side.

Sauce:

1 (12 ounce) jar seedless
    raspberry preserves   340 g
½ cup barbecue sauce   85 g
2 tablespoons raspberry
    vinegar   30 ml
2 tablespoons dijon-style
    mustard   30 g

- While chicken cooks, combine all sauce ingredients in bowl.

- Baste chicken with sauce during last 2 minutes of cooking. Serves 4.

You can figure about ¼ to ⅓ pound boneless chicken for an individual serving. One pound of boneless, skinless chicken breast will yield about 2 cups cooked meat. When you buy a whole chicken, you can figure 1 cup cooked chicken for each pound of whole chicken. One 3 pound chicken will yield about 3 cups cooked chicken.

Brown Rice Chicken

2 (5 ounce) cans premium chunk chicken breasts   2 (145 g)
2 (8.8 ounce) packages whole-grain brown ready rice   2 (255 g)
⅔ cup sun-dried tomatoes   35 g
2 ripe avocados, peeled, diced
¾ cup dijon-style mustard vinaigrette dressing   175 ml

- Pour broth from chicken into small bowl and save. Separate chicken into chunks. Prepare rice according to package directions.

- Combine chicken, rice, tomatoes and avocado in bowl.

- In separate bowl, combine vinaigrette dressing and ½ teaspoon (2 ml) salt.

- Gently stir into chicken-rice mixture and refrigerate for 2 hours before serving. Serves 6.

TIP: This rice goes in the microwave and is ready in 90 seconds. Not bad for the rush hour!

Sweet-Spicy Chicken Thighs

3 tablespoons chili powder	45 ml
3 tablespoon honey	50 g
2 tablespoon lemon juice	30 ml
10 - 12 chicken thighs	

- Preheat oven to 425° (220° C).

- Line 10 x 15-inch (25 x 38 cm) shallow baking pan with heavy foil and set metal rack in pan.

- Combine chili powder, honey, lemon juice and lots of salt and pepper in bowl.

- Brush mixture over chicken thighs and place on rack in baking pan. Turn thighs to coat completely.

- Bake, turning over once for about 35 minutes. Serves 5 to 6.

Jambalaya

1 (8 ounce) package jambalaya mix	230 g
1 (6 ounce) package frozen chicken breast strips, thawed	170 g
1 (11 ounce) can Mexicorn®	310 g
1 (2 ounce) can chopped black olives	60 g

- Combine jambalaya mix and 2¼ cups (560 g) water in soup or large saucepan. Heat to boiling, reduce heat and cook slowly for 5 minutes.

- Add chopped chicken, corn and black olives. Heat to boiling, reduce heat and simmer for about 20 minutes. Serves 4.

TIP: You could also add leftover ham or sausage and 1 tablespoon (15 ml) lemon juice to change it up some.

Chicken and Noodles

1 (3 ounce) package
   chicken-flavored,
   instant ramen noodles 85 g
1 (16 ounce) package
   frozen broccoli,
   cauliflower and
   carrots   455 g
⅔ cup sweet-and-sour
   sauce   180 g
3 boneless, skinless
   chicken breast halves,
   cooked

- Cook noodles and vegetables in saucepan with 2 cups (500 ml) boiling water for 3 minutes, stir occasionally and drain.

- Combine noodle-vegetable mixture with seasoning packet, sweet-and-sour sauce and a little salt and pepper. Cut chicken in strips, add chicken to noodle mixture and heat thoroughly. Serves 6.

TIP: You may want to add
     1 tablespoon (15 ml) soy
     sauce, if you have it on hand.

When you wash lettuce and greens for a salad, be
sure to dry the leaves between paper towels. Dressing
will be watered down if water is left on the leaves.

Favorite Oven-Fried Chicken

Marinade:

2 cups buttermilk	500 ml
2 tablespoons dijon-style mustard	30 g
2 teaspoons garlic powder	10 ml
1 teaspoon cayenne pepper	5 ml

Chicken:

6 boneless, skinless chicken breast halves	
2½ cups crushed corn flakes	70 g
¾ cup breadcrumbs	45 g
2 tablespoons olive oil	30 ml

- Combine marinade mixture in large bowl and mix well. Place chicken pieces in bowl and turn to coat well. Place in refrigerator and marinate for 2 hours or overnight.

- When ready to bake, preheat oven to 400° (205° C).

- Line large baking pan with foil and spray with cooking oil.

- Combine crushed corn flakes and breadcrumbs in large shallow bowl. Drizzle oil over crumbs and toss until they coat well.

- Take 1 piece chicken at a time, remove from marinade and dredge in crumb mixture. Press crumbs onto all sides of chicken and place in baking pan. Do not let sides touch. Bake for 35 to 40 minutes. Serves 6.

TIP: The easiest way to crush corn flakes is in a sealed plastic bag and the palm of your hand. You don't even have to get out the rolling pin if you don't want to or don't have one. Who needs a rolling pin anyway?

Super Chicken Spaghetti

This recipe is a little different twist on the always-popular chicken spaghetti. This is a wonderful casserole to serve to family or for company. It has great flavor with chicken, pasta and colorful vegetables all in one dish. It's a winner, I promise!

1 bunch fresh green onions and tops, chopped	
1 cup chopped celery	**100 g**
1 red bell pepper, chopped	
1 yellow or orange bell pepper, seeded, chopped	
¼ cup (½ stick) butter	**60 g**
1 tablespoon dried cilantro leaves	**15 ml**
1 teaspoon Italian seasoning	**5 ml**
1 (8 ounce) package thin spaghetti, cooked, drained	**230 g**
4 cups cooked, chopped chicken or turkey	**560 g**
1 (8 ounce) carton sour cream	**230 g**
1 (16 ounce) jar creamy alfredo sauce	**455 g**
1 (10 ounce) box frozen green peas, thawed	**280 g**
1 (8 ounce) package shredded mozzarella cheese, divided	**230 g**

- Preheat oven to 350° (175° C).

- Saute onions, celery and bell peppers in butter in large skillet. Combine onion-pepper mixture, cilantro, Italian seasoning, spaghetti, chicken, sour cream and alfredo sauce in large bowl and mix well.

- Sprinkle a little salt and pepper in mixture. Fold in peas and half mozzarella cheese. Spoon into sprayed 10 x 15-inch (25 cm x 38 cm) deep baking dish. Cover and bake for 45 minutes. Remove from oven and sprinkle remaining cheese over casserole. Return to oven for about 5 minutes. Serves 10.

Cornish Hens with Ginger-Orange Glaze

Glaze:

1 cup fresh orange juice	250 ml
2 tablespoons peeled, minced fresh ginger	30 ml
1 tablespoon soy sauce	15 ml
3 tablespoons honey	50 g

Cornish Hens:

2 (1½ pounds) cornish hens, halved	2 (680 g)
½ teaspoon ground ginger	2 ml

- Preheat oven to 450˚. (230° C).

- Combine orange juice, minced ginger, soy sauce and honey in saucepan and cook on high heat, stirring constantly for 3 minutes or until thick and glossy.

- Place hens in sprayed baking pan and sprinkle ground ginger and ½ teaspoon (2 ml) each of salt and pepper over birds.

- Spoon glaze mixture over hens and bake for 25 minutes. Brush glaze over hens several times during cooking. Serves 4.

Spinach and other leafy greens are loaded with lutein, a phytochemical that travels through the bloodstream to the eye. According to Tufts Center on Aging, lutein seems to absorb the type of light that can cause macular degeneration and may prevent cataracts. According to the University of California, Los Angeles, high levels of lutein in the bloodstream may prevent fatty deposits from clogging arteries, as well.

Turkey Cassoulet

*This is a great recipe
for leftover turkey.*

½ pound smoked turkey sausage	230 g
2 cups cooked, cubed turkey	280 g
3 carrots, sliced	
1 onion, halved, sliced	
1 (15 ounce) can navy bean	425 g
1 (15 ounce) white lima beans	425 g
1 (8 ounce) can tomato sauce	230 g
1 teaspoon dried thyme	5 ml
¼ teaspoon ground allspice	1 ml

- Cut turkey sausage in ½-inch (1.2 cm) pieces. Combine all ingredients in sprayed slow cooker. Cover and cook on LOW for 4 to 5 hours. Serves 6.

Turkey and Rice Olé

*This may be served as a one-dish
meal or as a sandwich wrap
in flour tortillas.*

1 pound ground turkey	455 g
1 (5.5 ounce) package Mexican rice mix	155 g
1 (15 ounce) can black beans, rinsed, drained	425 g
1 cup thick-and-chunky salsa	265 g

- Brown turkey in large skillet and break up large pieces with fork. Add rice mix and 2 cups (500 ml) water.

- Bring to a boil, reduce heat and simmer for about 8 minutes or until rice is tender. Stir in beans and salsa and cook just until mixture heats through. Serves 6.

Turkey and Ham Tetrazzini

This is another old-fashioned dish modified for today's "hurry-up meal", but it keeps the same great taste.

½ cup slivered almonds, toasted	85 g
1 (10 ounce) can cream of mushroom soup	280 g
1 (10 ounce) can cream of chicken soup	280 g
¾ cup milk	175 ml
2 tablespoons dry white wine	30 ml
1 (8 ounce) box thin spaghetti, cooked, drained	230 g
2½ cups cooked, diced turkey	350 g
2 cups cooked, diced ham	280 g
½ cup chopped green bell pepper	75 g
½ cup chopped red bell pepper	75 g
½ cup halved pitted ripe olives	65 g
1 (8 ounce) package shredded cheddar cheese	230 g

• Preheat oven to 350° (175° C).

• Mix almonds, soups, milk and wine in large bowl. Stir in spaghetti, turkey, ham, bell peppers and olives. Spoon into sprayed 9 x 13-inch (23 x 33 cm) baking dish.

• Cover and bake for 35 minutes or until casserole is hot and bubbly. Uncover and sprinkle top of casserole with cheese. Return to oven for 5 minutes. Serves 6 to 8.

Turkey-Asparagus Alfredo

1 bunch fresh asparagus
1 red bell pepper, seeded,
   thinly sliced
½ pound deli smoked
   turkey   **230 g**
1 (16 ounce) carton
   alfredo sauce   **455 g**
Rice, cooked

- Bring ½ cup (125 ml) water in skillet to a boil. Cut off woody ends of asparagus and cut into thirds.

- Add asparagus and bell peppers, cook on medium-high heat for 4 minutes or until tender-crisp and drain.

- Sliced turkey in thin strips. With skillet still on medium-high heat, stir in alfredo sauce and turkey strips.

- Bring to a boil, reduce heat and simmer until mixture heats thoroughly. Serve over rice. Serves 4.

Pears in the grocery store are usually green and hard because they ripen off the tree. The best way for them to ripen is stored in a paper bag at room temperature until the flesh at the neck gives a little when you press against it. Once ripe they should be stored in the coldest part of the refrigerator.

Caribbean Turkey

Turkey tenderloins are wonderful. You will be glad you cooked them!

2 tablespoons jerk
    seasoning   30 ml
1½ - 2 pounds turkey
    tenderloins   680 g - 1.2 kg
1 tablespoons fresh
    chopped rosemary   15 ml
1½ cups raspberry-
    chipotle sauce,
    divided   410 g
Potatoes, mashed

- Rub jerk seasoning evenly over tenderloins, sprinkle with rosemary and press into tenderloins. Cover and refrigerate for 1 to 2 hours.

- Grill tenderloins with lid closed over medium-high heat for 5 to 10 minutes on each side. Baste with half raspberry-chipotle sauce.

- Let tenderloin stand for 10 minutes before slicing and serve with remaining raspberry-chipotle sauce. Serve over mashed potatoes. Serves 6.

If you need a large turkey, consider buying two smaller turkeys instead of one large one. It doubles the number of legs, breasts, thighs, giblets and you have shorter cooking time.

Turkey Pasta

3 ounces twisted noodles	85 g
1 (.04 ounce) package ranch salad dressing mix	10 g
¾ cup mayonnaise	170 g
1 cup milk	250 ml
3 cups cooked, diced turkey	420 g
1 (10 ounce) package frozen peas	280 g
1 (4 ounce) can chopped green chilies	115 g
¾ cup cracker crumbs	45 g

- Preheat oven to 350° (175° C).

- Cook noodles according to package directions. Drain.

- Combine salad dressing mix, mayonnaise and milk in large bowl. Add turkey, peas and green chilies and mix well.

- Add noodles to turkey mixture; toss. Pour into sprayed 3-quart (3 L) baking dish.

- Cover and bake for 25 minutes. Uncover and sprinkle cracker crumbs over top of casserole. Return to oven for additional 10 to 15 minutes. Serves 5 to 6.

For all the information you ever wanted to know about turkeys, call the Butterball Turkey Talk-Line at 1-800-BUTTERBALL (1-800-288-8372). While the Turkey Talk-Line is open during November and December, customer assistance at the same number provides help year round.

Powerful Pork

Dipped, Smothered, Noodled and Chopped

Powerful Pork Contents

Pork Tenderloin with Cranberry Sauce

2 (1 pound) pork tenderloins	2 (455 g)
½ cup chopped fresh cilantro	10 g
½ teaspoon ground cumin	2 ml
2 teaspoons minced garlic	10 ml

- Preheat oven to 375° (190° C).

- Season tenderloin with a little salt and pepper, cilantro, cumin and garlic.

- Place in foil-lined baking pan and bake for 15 minutes. Reduce heat to 325° (160° C) and bake for additional 35 minutes. Slice to serve.

Sauce:

1 (16 ounce) can whole cranberries	455 g
1 cup orange marmalade	320 g
1 (8 ounce) can crushed pineapple, drained	170 g
¾ cup chopped pecans	85 g

- Combine cranberries, marmalade, pineapple and pecans in bowl and serve with tenderloin. Sauce may be served at room temperature or warmed. Serves 8.

Grilled Pork Tenderloin with Rice and Beans

2 (1 pound) pork
  tenderloins   2 (455 g)
1 tablespoon canola
  oil   15 ml
2 tablespoons jerk
  seasoning   30 ml

- Rub tenderloins with oil and sprinkle with jerk seasoning.

- Grill over medium-high heat for about 25 minutes, brown on both sides and cook until meat thermometer inserted in center registers 160° (70° C).

Rice and Beans:

1 (6 ounce) package
  chicken-flavored rice   170 g
1 (15 ounce) can black
  beans, rinsed   425 g
½ cup roasted red bell
  pepper, sliced   70 g
2 tablespoons chopped
  cilantro   2 g

- Cook rice according to package directions and add beans, bell pepper, cilantro and a little salt and pepper.

- Spoon on serving platter.

- Slice tenderloin and arrange on top of rice-bean mixture. Serves 8.

It is best for cooked pork to have an internal temperature of 150° to 160° to yield the juiciest and most tender meat. Higher internal temperatures lead to dry, overcooked pork. The best way to check for doneness is to use a meat thermometer.

Fiesta Pork Casserole

This zesty casserole is so easy to put together and it really gets your attention! It is an especially nice change of pace from the usual Mexican dish with ground beef.

2 pounds boneless pork tenderloin, cut into 1-inch cubes	910 g/2.5 cm
1 onion, chopped	
1 green bell pepper, seeded, chopped	
3 tablespoons canola oil	45 ml
1 (15 ounce) can black beans, rinsed, drained	425 g
1 (10 ounce) can fiesta nacho cheese soup	280 g
1 (15 ounce) can stewed tomatoes	425 g
1 (4 ounce) can chopped green chilies	115 g
1 cup instant brown rice, cooked	195 g
¾ cup salsa	200 g
2 teaspoons ground cumin	10 ml
½ teaspoon garlic powder	2 ml
¾ cup shredded Mexican 3-cheese blend	85 g

- Preheat oven to 350° (175° C).

- Brown and cook pork, onion and bell pepper in oil in very large skillet until pork is no longer pink. Drain.

- Add beans, fiesta nacho cheese soup, stewed tomatoes, green chilies, rice, salsa, cumin, ½ teaspoon (2 ml) salt and garlic powder to skillet. Cook on medium heat, stirring occasionally, until mixture bubbles.

- Spoon into sprayed 4-quart (4 L) baking dish. Bake for 30 minutes or until bubbly around edges. Remove from oven and sprinkle with cheese. Let stand a few minutes before serving. Serves 8 to 10.

One-Dish Pork and Peas

So many of our casseroles are chicken, but pork is so good and always tender. This blend of ingredients makes a delicious dish.

1½ pounds pork tenderloin, cut into ½-inch (1.2 cm) cubes	680 g
2 tablespoons canola oil	30 ml
1 cup sliced celery	100 g
1 onion, chopped	
1 red bell pepper, seeded, chopped	
1 (8 ounce) package small egg noodles, cooked, drained	230 g
1 (10 ounce) can cream of chicken soup	280 g
½ cup half-and-half cream	155 g
1 (10 ounce) package frozen green peas, thawed	280 g
1 cup seasoned breadcrumbs	120 g
⅓ cup chopped walnuts	130 g

- Preheat oven to 350° (175° C).

- Brown cubed pork in oil in large skillet. Reduce heat and cook for about 20 minutes. Remove pork to separate dish.

- In remaining oil, saute celery, onion and bell pepper. Add pork, noodles, soup, half-and-half cream, peas, 1 teaspoon (5 ml) salt and ½ teaspoon (2 ml) pepper.

- Spoon into sprayed 3-quart (3 L) baking dish. Sprinkle with breadcrumbs and walnuts.

- Bake for about 25 minutes or until bubbly. Serves 8.

Pork and Noodles Supreme

2 tablespoons canola oil   30 ml
2 pounds pork
   tenderloin, cut
   into 1-inch cubes 910 g/2.5 cm
2 ribs celery, chopped
1 red bell pepper,
   seeded, chopped
1 green bell pepper,
   seeded, chopped
1 onion, chopped
1 (12 ounce) package
   medium egg noodles,
   cooked, drained   340 g
1 (10 ounce) can cream
   of celery soup   280 g
1 (10 ounce) can cream
   of chicken soup   280 g
1 (15 ounce) can
   cream-style corn   425 g
¾ cup half-and-half
   cream   235 g
1½ cups crushed
   corn flakes   45 g
3 tablespoons butter,
   melted   35 g

- Preheat oven to 350° (175° C).

- Heat oil in skillet and brown and cook pork for about 15 minutes. Place pork into large bowl.

- With remaining oil in skillet, saute celery, bell peppers and onion. Spoon into bowl with pork. Add noodles, both soups, creamed corn, half-and-half cream and ½ teaspoon (2 ml) each salt and pepper to pork.

- Mix well and pour into sprayed 9 x 13-inch (23 x 33 cm) baking dish.

- Combine crushed corn flakes and butter in bowl and sprinkle over casserole. Cover and bake for about 30 minutes. Serves 8.

TIP: If it's hard to find a 1½-pound (680 g) pork roast, buy 2 (¾-pound/340 g) pork tenderloins. It is a little more expensive, but well worth it because you are not buying bones and the tenderloin will be tender and delicious.

Oodles of Noodles

1½ - 2 pounds pork
   tenderloin, cut
   into 1-inch
   (2.5 cm) cubes   680 - 910 g
3 tablespoons canola oil   45 ml
2 cups chopped celery   200 g
1 red bell pepper, seeded,
   chopped
1 green bell pepper,
   seeded, chopped
1 onion, chopped
1 (4 ounce) can sliced
   mushrooms   115 g
1 (10 ounce) can tomatoes
   and green chilies   280 ml
1 (10 ounce) can cream
   of mushroom soup
   with garlic   280 ml
1 (10 ounce) can cream
   of celery soup   280 ml
¼ cup soy sauce   60 ml
1 (8 ounce) package
   elbow macaroni,
   cooked, drained   230 g
2 cups chow mein noodles 110 g

- Preheat oven to 350° (175° C).

- Brown pork in oil in skillet and cook on low heat for about 15 minutes. Remove pork with slotted spoon to side dish.

- Saute celery, bell peppers and onion in same skillet in remaining oil. Combine pork, celery-onion mixture, mushrooms, tomatoes and green chilies, soups, soy sauce and macaroni in large bowl.

- Spoon into sprayed 9 x 13-inch (23 x 33 cm) baking dish or 2 smaller baking dishes. Top with chow mein noodles. Bake for 50 minutes. Serves 8 to 10.

TIP: If you make 2 smaller casseroles, you may freeze one. Wait to sprinkle the chow mein noodles over casserole until just before you place it in the oven to bake.

Sweet Peach Pork Tenderloin

3 tablespoons
  dijon-style
  mustard   40 g
1 tablespoon soy
  sauce   15 ml
1 (12 ounce) jar peach
  preserves   340 g
2 (1 pound) pork
  tenderloins   2 (455 g)

- Preheat oven to 325° (160° C).

- Combine mustard, soy sauce and peach preserves in saucepan. Heat and stir just until mixture blends.

- Place tenderloins in sprayed baking pan and spoon peach mixture over top.

- Sprinkle a little salt and pepper over tenderloin.

- Cover pan with foil and bake for 1 hour and remove from oven.

- Remove from oven and let stand for about 10 minutes before slicing. Serves 8.

Pork Chop Supper

1 (18 ounce) package
  smoked pork chops   510 g
Canola oil
1 (12 ounce) jar pork
  gravy   240 g
¼ cup milk   60 ml
1 (15 ounce) can small
  new potatoes   425 g

- Brown pork chops in large skillet with a little oil. Pour gravy and milk or water into skillet and stir mixture around chops until they mix well.

- Add new potatoes around chops and gravy. Place lid on skillet and simmer on medium-low heat for about 15 minutes or until potatoes are tender. Serves 6.

TIP: The (18 ounce/510 g) package pork chops will give you about 5 to 6 chops if they are of average size.

Sweet Potato Ham

1 (16 ounce) ½-inch
thick, fully cooked
ham slice   455 g/1.2 cm
1 (18 ounce) can
sweet potatoes,
drained   510 g
½ cup packed brown
sugar   110 g
⅓ cup chopped
pecans   40 g

- Preheat oven to 350° (175° C).

- Cut outer edge of ham fat at
  1-inch (2.5 cm) intervals to
  prevent curling, but do not cut
  into ham.

- Place on 10-inch (25 cm)
  microwave-safe pie pan and
  broil with top 5 inches (13 cm)
  from heat for 5 minutes.

- Mash each piece of sweet
  potatoes in bowl with fork just
  once (not totally mashed) and
  add brown sugar, a little salt and
  chopped pecans and mix well.

- Spoon mixture over ham slice
  and cook for about 15 minutes.
  Serve right from microwave-safe
  pie pan. Serves 6.

*When buying a ham, the terms "water added"
and "natural juices added" mean that you are
paying for the water weight added to the ham.*

Pork Chop Casserole

6 (¾-inch thick)
  boneless pork
  chops   6 (1.8 cm)
2 tablespoons canola
  oil   30 ml
1 green bell pepper
1 yellow bell pepper,
  seeded, chopped
1 (15 ounce) can
  tomato sauce   425 g
1 (15 ounce) can
  Italian stewed
  tomatoes   425 g
1 teaspoon minced
  garlic   5 ml
1½ cups long grain
  rice   280 g

- Preheat oven to 350° (175° C).

- Sprinkle pork chops with about ½ teaspoon (2 ml) each of salt and pepper. Brown pork chops in oil in skillet. Remove chops from skillet and set aside.

- Cut top off green bell pepper, remove seeds, cut 6 rings from green bell pepper and set aside. Combine yellow bell pepper, tomato sauce, stewed tomatoes, 1 cup (250 ml) water, garlic and ½ teaspoon (2 ml) salt in separate bowl and stir well.

- Spread rice in sprayed 9 x 13-inch (23 x 33 cm) baking dish and slowly pour tomato mixture over rice. Arrange pork chops over rice and place pepper ring over each chop. Cover and bake for 1 hour or until chops and rice are tender. Serves 6.

Easy Pork Stew

This is great with cornbread!

2 (1 pound) pork
    tenderloins, cubed 2 (455 g)
2 (12 ounce) jars pork
    gravy   2 (340 g)
¼ cup chili sauce   70 g
1 (16 ounce) package
    frozen stew
    vegetables,
    thawed   455 g

- Cook pork pieces in sprayed soup pot on medium-high heat for 10 minutes, stirring frequently.

- Stir in gravy, chili sauce and stew vegetables and bring to a boil. Reduce heat and simmer for 12 minutes or until vegetables are tender. Serves 4.

Parmesan Covered Pork Chops

½ cup grated parmesan
    cheese   120 ml
⅔ cup Italian seasoned
    breadcrumbs   160 ml
1 egg
4 - 5 thin-cut pork chops
Canola oil

- Combine cheese and breadcrumbs in shallow bowl. Beat egg with 1 teaspoon (5 ml) water on shallow plate.

- Dip each pork chop in beaten egg then into breadcrumb mixture.

- Cook over medium-high heat in skillet with a little oil for about 5 minutes on each side or until golden brown. Serves 4 to 5.

Marinated Garlic-Herb Tenderloin

2 (1 pound) pork
  tenderloins   2 (455 g)
1 (12 ounce) bottle
  roasted garlic-herb
  marinade, divided 340 g
1 (8 ounce) package
  medium egg
  noodles   230 g
¼ cup (½ stick) butter 60 g

- Butterfly pork lengthwise, being careful not to cut all the way through. Press open to flatten and place in large resealable plastic bag. Pour ¾ cup (190 g) marinade into bag and close top securely. Marinate for 25 minutes and turn several times.

- Grill 4 to 5 inches (10 cm) from hot coals for 8 minutes.

- Turn pork over and brush with additional marinade and cook for an additional 8 minutes.

- Cook noodles according to package directions with butter. When ready to serve place pork chops over noodles. Serves 8.

Heating a fully cooked ham is the best way
to bring out the flavors and tenderness.

Pork Chops with Black Bean Salsa

2 teaspoons chili powder   10 ml
2 tablespoons canola oil   30 ml
6 boneless thin-cut pork
  chops

- Combine chili powder and
  ½ teaspoon (2 ml) salt in
  bowl. Rub oil over pork chops
  and rub chili powder mixture
  over chops.

- Place in skillet over medium
  heat and cook pork chops for
  about 5 minutes on both sides.

Salsa:

1 (15 ounce) can black
  beans, rinsed, drained 425 g
1 (24 ounce) jar
  refrigerated citrus
  fruit, drained   680 g
1 ripe avocado, sliced
⅔ cup Italian salad
  dressing   150 ml

- Combine beans, fruit and
  avocado in bowl and toss with
  salad dressing. Serve with pork
  chops. Serves 6.

Be careful not to overcook thin pork chops.
Cook slowly over medium to low heat.

Onion-Smothered Pork Chops

6 (½-inch thick) pork
   chops   6 (1.2 cm)
1 tablespoon canola
   oil   15 ml
2 tablespoons butter   30 ml
1 onion, chopped
1 (10 ounce) can
   cream of onion
   soup   280 ml
Brown rice, cooked

- Preheat oven to 325° (160° C).

- Brown pork chops in oil in skillet, simmer for about 10 minutes and place pork chops in sprayed shallow baking pan.

- Add butter in same skillet and saute onion. (Pan juices are brown from pork chops so onions will be brown.)

- Add onion soup and ½ cup (125 ml) water and stir well. (Sauce will have a pretty, light brown color.)

- Pour onion soup mixture over pork chops.

- Cover and bake for 40 minutes and serve over brown rice. Serves 6.

You should trim about ¼ to ½ inch off the fat on the outside of a ham before you spread the glaze on it.

Pork-Potato Chop

6 boneless or loin pork
  chops
Canola oil
1 (14 ounce) can
  chicken broth   400 g
2 (1 ounce) packets
  dry onion gravy
  mix   2 (30 g)
4 new (red) potatoes,
  sliced

- Seasoned chops with a little salt and pepper and brown in large skillet with a little oil. Combine chicken broth and gravy mix in bowl. Add potatoes to skillet with pork chops and cover with gravy mixture.

- Heat to boil, cover and simmer for 45 minutes or until pork chops and potatoes are fork-tender. Serves 6.

Pork Chops and Gravy

6 (½-inch thick) pork
  chops   6 (1.2 cm)
8 - 10 new (red)
  potatoes with
  peels, quartered
1 (16 ounce) package
  baby carrots   455 g
2 (10 ounce) cans
  cream of
  mushroom soup
  with roasted garlic 2 (280 g)

- Sprinkle a little salt and pepper on pork chops.

- Brown pork chops in skillet and place in 5 to 6-quart (5 to 6 L) slow cooker. Place potatoes and carrots around pork chops.

- Heat mushroom soup with ½ cup (125 ml) water in saucepan and pour over chops and vegetables.

- Cover and cook in slow cooker on LOW for 6 to 7 hours. Serves 6.

Pork Chops, Potatoes and Green Beans

**6 - 8 boneless or loin
    pork chops**
**2 (15 ounce) cans white
    potatoes, drained   2 (425 g)**
**2 (15 ounce) cans cut
    green beans,
    drained   2 (425 g)**

- Season pork chops with salt and pepper, if desired and brown pork chops in large non-stick heavy pan over medium heat.

- Pour gravy over pork chops. Cover and simmer for 30 minutes.

- Add potatoes and green beans and simmer for about 10 minutes or until pork chops are tender and green beans and potatoes are hot. Serve with tossed green salad. Serves 6.

Uncle Ben's Ham and Rice

**1 (7 ounce) box brown
    and wild rice-
    mushroom recipe   200 g**
**3 - 4 cups cooked,
    chopped or cubed
    ham   420 - 560 g**
**1 (4 ounce) can sliced
    mushrooms,
    drained   115 g**
**1 (10 ounce) package
    frozen green peas   280 g**
2 cups chopped celery 200 g

- Combine rice, seasoning packet, ham, mushrooms, peas, celery plus 2⅔ cups (650 ml) water in 4 to 5-quart (4 to 5 L) slow cooker. Stir to mix well.

- Cover and cook in slow cooker on LOW for 2 to 4 hours. Serves 6.

Ham-It-Up Supper

This is really simple to put together and the kids will be ready to eat their vegetables when ham and cheese are in the picture.

1 (6 ounce) package instant long grain-wild rice	170 g
1 (10 ounce) package frozen broccoli spears, thawed	280 g
1 (8 ounce) can whole kernel corn, drained	230 g
3 cups cooked, cubed ham	420 g
1 (10 ounce) can cream of mushroom soup	280 g
1 cup mayonnaise	225 g
1 teaspoon mustard	5 ml
1 cup shredded cheddar cheese	115 g
1 (3 ounce) can fried onion rings	85 g

- Preheat oven to 350° (175° C).

- Prepare rice according to package directions.

- Spoon into sprayed 3-quart (3 L) baking dish. Top with broccoli, corn and ham.

- Combine soup, mayonnaise, mustard, shredded cheese and ½ teaspoon (2 ml) each of salt and pepper in saucepan and mix well. Spread over top of rice-ham mixture.

- Cover and bake for about 30 minutes. Uncover and sprinkle onion rings over bake for additional 15 minutes or until casserole is bubbly around edges and onion rings are light brown. Serves 8.

TIP: What a great way to use leftover ham, all the little slivers and chunks left from those nice big slices.

Fruit-Covered Ham Slice

2 (15 ounce) cans fruit cocktail, with juice	2 (425 g)
½ cup packed brown sugar	110 g
2 tablespoons cornstarch	15 g
1 (½-inch thick) center-cut ham slice	1.2 cm

- Combine fruit cocktail, brown sugar and cornstarch in saucepan and mix well. Cook on medium heat, stirring frequently, until sauce thickens.

- Place ham slice in large non-stick skillet on medium heat. Cook for about 5 minutes or just until ham thoroughly heats.

- Place on serving platter and spoon fruit sauce over ham.

Peach Glazed Ham

1 (5 pound) boneless ham	2.3 kg
1 (16 ounce) jar peach preserves	455 g
3 tablespoons dijon-style mustard	40 g
¼ cup packed brown sugar	55 g

- Cook ham according to package directions. Combine preserves, mustard and brown sugar in bowl and mix well.

- About 30 minutes before cooking time ends, remove ham from oven and drain any liquid.

- Brush ham with preserve-sugar mixture and return to oven for 30 minutes.

- Heat remaining preserve-sugar mixture in saucepan. Serve ham with heated preserve-sugar mixture. Serves 8.

Noodles and Ham with Veggies

1 (8 ounce) package medium egg noodles	230 g
1 (10 ounce) can cream of celery soup	280 g
1 (10 ounce) can cream of broccoli soup	280 g
1 teaspoon chicken bouillon granules	5 ml
1½ cups half-and-half cream	470 g
1 (8 ounce) can whole kernel corn, drained	230 g
1 (16 ounce) package frozen broccoli, cauliflower and carrots, thawed	455 g
3 cups cooked, cubed ham	420 g
1 (8 ounce) package shredded cheddar-Jack cheese, divided	230 g

- Preheat oven to 350° (175° C).

- Cook noodles according to package directions and drain.

- Combine soups, chicken bouillon, half-and-half cream, corn, broccoli-carrot mixture, ham, ½ teaspoon (2 ml) salt and 1 teaspoon (5 ml) pepper in large bowl and mix well.

- Fold in egg noodles and half cheese. Spoon into sprayed 9 x 13-inch (23 x 33 cm) baking dish. Cover and bake for 45 minutes.

- Uncover and sprinkle remaining cheese over top of casserole. Return to oven and bake for additional 5 minutes or until cheese is bubbly. Serves 8.

Ham and Potatoes Olé!

1 (24 ounce) package frozen hash browns with onions and peppers, thawed	680 g
3 cups cooked, cubed ham	420 g
1 (10 ounce) can cream of chicken soup	280 g
1 (10 ounce) can fiesta nacho cheese soup	280 g
1 cup hot salsa	265 g
1 (8 ounce) package shredded cheddar-Jack cheese	230 g

- Preheat oven to 350° (175° C).

- Combine potatoes, ham, both soups and salsa in large bowl and mix well. Spoon into sprayed 9 x 13-inch (23 x 33 cm) baking dish.

- Cover and bake for 40 minutes. Uncover and sprinkle cheese over casserole and bake for additional 5 minutes. Serves 8.

Supper in a Dish

2 (9 ounce) packages rice boil-in-a-bag	2 (255 g)
3 cups cooked, cubed ham	420 g
1½ cups shredded cheddar cheese	170 g
1 (8 ounce) can green peas, drained	230 g

- Preheat oven to 350° (175° C).

- Prepare rice according to package directions. Combine rice, ham, cheese and peas in large bowl.

- Pour into 3-quart (3 L) baking dish and bake for 15 to 20 minutes. Serves 6.

Tortellini-Ham Supper

*This is another great
recipe for leftover ham.*

2 (9 ounce) packages refrigerated tortellini	2 (255 g)
1 (10 ounce) package frozen green peas, thawed	280 g
1 (16 ounce) jar alfredo sauce	455 g
3 cups cooked, cubed ham	420 g

- Cook tortellini according to package directions. Add green peas for about 5 minutes before tortellini is done and drain.

- Combine alfredo sauce and ham in saucepan and heat until thoroughly hot. Toss with tortellini and peas. Serve immediately. Serves 6 to 8.

Ham and Sweet Potatoes

¼ cup dijon-style mustard, divided	60 g
1 (3 - 4 pounds) boneless smoked ham	1.4 - 1.8 kg
½ cup honey or packed brown sugar	170 g/110 g
1 (29 ounce) can sweet potatoes, drained	805 g

- Preheat oven to 325° (160° C).

- Spread half mustard on ham. Place ham in sprayed shallow baking pan and bake for 20 minutes.

- Combine remaining mustard with honey or brown sugar in bowl and spread over ham. Add sweet potatoes and bake for 20 minutes. Serves 6.

Broiled Ham with Sweet Potatoes

1 (½-inch thick) fully
   cooked, center-cut
   ham slice   1 (1.2 cm)
1 (15 ounce) can sweet
   potatoes, drained   425 g
½ cup packed brown
   sugar   110 g
2 tablespoons butter,
   melted   30 g
1 teaspoon ground
   cinnamon   5 ml

- Cut edges of ham fat at 1-inch (2.5 cm) intervals to prevent curling. Place ham on broiler pan and broil for about 5 minutes.

- Spoon sweet potatoes into shallow dish, mash with fork and stir in brown sugar, butter and cinnamon.

- Spoon sweet potato mixture over ham and place under broiler. Broil for about 5 minutes or until sweet potatoes are hot, brown and tender. Serves 4 to 6.

Ham and Veggies

2 (15 ounce) cans
   mixed vegetables   2 (425 g)
1 (10 ounce) can
   cream of celery
   soup   280 g
2 cups cooked, cubed
   ham   280 g
½ teaspoon dried
   basil   2 ml

- Cook vegetables according to package directions. Add soup, ham and basil.

- Cook until mixture heats well and serve hot. Serves 6.

Bow-Tie Pasta with Ham and Veggies

*This is a great way
to use leftover ham.*

1 (8 ounce) package bow-tie (farfalle) pasta	230 g
1 (10 ounce) package frozen broccoli florets, thawed	280 g
1 (10 ounce) package frozen green peas, thawed	280 g
1 (16 ounce) jar alfredo sauce	455 g
1 pound cooked, cubed ham	455 g

- Cook pasta according to package directions in large saucepan. Add broccoli and peas during last 3 minutes of cooking time. Drain well.

- Add alfredo sauce and ham. Cook and stir gently over very low heat to keep ingredients from sticking to pan. Pour into serving bowl. Serves 6 to 8.

German-Style Ribs and Kraut

3 - 4 pounds baby-back pork ribs or country-style pork ribs, trimmed   1.4 - 1.8 kg
3 potatoes, peeled, cubed or sliced
1 (32 ounce) jar refrigerated sauerkraut, drained   910 g
¼ cup pine nuts, toasted   30 g

- Brown ribs on all sides in large, sprayed heavy pan. Add a little pepper and 1 cup (250 ml) water. Bring to a boil, reduce heat and simmer for 2 hours or until ribs are very tender.

- Add potatoes and cook on low heat for 20 minutes. Add sauerkraut and continue cooking until potatoes are done.

- Sprinkle pine nuts on ribs and kraut immediately before serving. Serves 6 to 8.

TIP: To toast pine nuts, place nuts in skillet on medium heat, and stir constantly, until golden brown. You may also put them on a baking sheet and cook at 300° (150° C) for 5 to 10 minutes.

Always save a ham bone for soups, stews and beans. If you don't need it immediately, just freeze it for later.

Oven-Roasted Baby-Backs

⅓ cup orange juice	75 ml
⅓ cup soy sauce	75 ml
1 teaspoon ground cumin	5 ml
½ cup packed brown sugar	110 g
2 - 3 pounds baby back pork ribs	910 g - 1.4 kg

- Combine orange juice, soy sauce, cumin and brown sugar in large resealable plastic bag. Shake or mash bag to blend thoroughly and to dissolve brown sugar.

- Cut ribs into individual ribs, add to bag and marinate for 1 to 2 hours.

- When ready to bake, preheat oven to 325° (160° C).

- Transfer ribs and marinade to shallow baking pan and arrange in 1 layer. Ribs should not touch.

- Bake for 45 minutes. Remove from oven, turn ribs with tongs and continue roasting for an additional 1 hour.

When you are frying ham steaks or thick slices, cut slits in the fat around the edges and the ham will not curl up around the edges.

Fettuccini Supreme

1 (16 ounce) package fettuccini	455 g
½ cup whipping cream	40 g
½ cup (1 stick) butter, sliced	115 g
½ teaspoon dried basil	2 ml
1 tablespoon dried parsley	15 ml
2 cups cooked, diced ham	280 g
1 cup grated parmesan cheese	100 g

- Cook fettuccini according to package directions and drain. Immediately place fettuccini back into saucepan.

- Add whipping cream, butter, basil, parsley, ham and ¼ teaspoon (1 ml) salt and toss until butter melts. Fold in parmesan cheese, pour into serving bowl and serve hot. Serves 8.

Creamy Potatoes and Ham

5 medium potatoes, peeled, sliced, divided	
1 teaspoon seasoned salt, divided	5 ml
1 onion, chopped, divided	
2 cups cooked, cubed ham, divided	280 g
1 (8 ounce) package cubed Velveeta® cheese, divided	230 g
1 (10 ounce) can broccoli cheese soup	280 g
¼ cup milk	60 ml

- Layer half each of potatoes, seasoned salt, onion, ham and cheese in slow cooker and repeat layer.

- Combine soup and milk in bowl until fairly smooth and pour over potato mixture. Cover and cook on HIGH for 1 hour. Reduce heat to LOW and cook for 6 to 7 hours. Serves 6.

Hot Pasta Frittata

½ cup chopped onion	80 g
1 green bell pepper, seeded, chopped	
1 red bell pepper, seeded, chopped	
3 tablespoons butter	35 g
1 (8 ounce) box thin spaghetti, slightly broken up, cooked	230 g
1½ cups shredded mozzarella cheese	170 g
5 eggs	
½ cup milk	125 ml
⅓ cup grated parmesan cheese	35 g
1 tablespoon basil	15 ml
1 teaspoon oregano	5 ml
2 cups cooked, diced ham	280 g

- Preheat oven to 375° (190° C).

- Saute onion and bell peppers in butter in skillet over medium heat for about 5 minutes, but do not brown.

- Combine onion-pepper mixture and spaghetti in large bowl and toss. Add mozzarella cheese and toss.

- In separate bowl, beat eggs, milk, parmesan cheese, basil, oregano, about ½ teaspoon salt and pepper. Add spaghetti mixture, ham and pour into sprayed 9 x 13-inch (23 x 33 cm) baking pan or 2-quart (2 L) baking dish.

- Cover and bake for 10 minutes. Uncover to make sure eggs are set. If not, bake for additional 2 to 3 minutes. Cut into squares and serve. Serves 8.

TIP: This can be prepared, refrigerated and baked later. Let it get to room temperature before heating.

Colorful Veggie-Ham Salad

4 cups fresh broccoli
florets   285 g
4 cups fresh cauliflower
florets   400 g
1 red onion, sliced
1 (4 ounce) can sliced
ripe olives   115 g
3 small zucchini, sliced
2 cups cooked, chopped
ham   280 g

- Combine broccoli, cauliflower, onion, olives, zucchini and ham in large bowl and toss.

Dressing:

1 (.04 ounce) packet zesty
Italian dressing mix   10 g
1½ cups bottled zesty
Italian salad dressing   375 ml
2 tablespoons extra-
virgin olive oil   30 ml

- Combine dry dressing mix, bottled dressing and olive oil in small bowl and mix well.

- Pour over vegetables and toss to coat. Refrigerate for several hours before serving or make 1 day in advance. Serves 6.

Good vegetable sources of vitamin C are tomatoes, peppers, broccoli and cauliflower.

Ham Salad I

3 cups cooked, chopped
    ham   420 g
1 bunch fresh green
    onions with tops,
    chopped
½ cup slivered almonds,
    toasted   85 g
½ cup sunflower seeds   65 g
2 cups chopped fresh
    broccoli florets   140 g
¾ cup mayonnaise   170 g
Lettuce leaves

- Combine ham, green onions, almonds, sunflower seeds and broccoli florets in bowl, toss with mayonnaise and refrigerate. Serve on lettuce leaves. Serves 4.

Ham Salad II

3 cups cooked, chopped
    ham   420 g
¾ cup chopped celery   75 g
1 cup small curd cottage
    cheese, drained   225 g
1 cup chopped cauliflower
    florets   100 g
1 cup chopped broccoli
    florets   70 g
Honey-mustard
    salad dressing
Lettuce leaves

- Combine ham, celery, cottage cheese, cauliflower and broccoli in bowl, toss with salad dressing and refrigerate. Serve on lettuce leaves. Serves 4.

Vegetable-Ham Chowder

A great recipe for leftover ham

1 medium potato
2 (10 ounce) cans
   cream of celery
   soup   2 (280 g)
1 (14 ounce) can
   chicken broth   400 g
3 cups cooked, diced
   ham   420 g
1 (15 ounce) can
   whole kernel corn   425 g
2 carrots, sliced
1 onion, coarsely
   chopped

1 teaspoon dried basil 5 ml
1 teaspoon seasoned
   salt   5 ml
1 teaspoon white
   pepper   5 ml
1 (10 ounce) package
   frozen broccoli
   florets   280 g

- Cut potato into 1-inch (2.5 cm) pieces. Combine all ingredients except broccoli florets in large slow cooker.

- Cover and cook on LOW for 5 to 6 hours. Add broccoli and ½ teaspoon (2 ml) salt to cooker and cook for additional 1 hour. Serves 4.

Large or firm vegetables like potatoes, onions and carrots cook more slowly than meat. Put these vegetables in the slow cooker first and put the meat on top of them.

Sandwich Souffle

A fun lunch!

Butter, softened
8 slices white bread
　　without crusts
4 slices ham
4 slices American cheese
2 cups milk　　　　　　500 ml
2 eggs, beaten

- Butter bread on both sides, make 4 sandwiches with ham and cheese. Place sandwiches in sprayed 8-inch (20 cm) square baking pan.

- Beat milk, eggs and a little salt and pepper in bowl. Pour over sandwiches and soak for 1 to 2 hours.

- When ready to bake, preheat oven to 350° (175° C).

- Bake for 45 to 50 minutes. Scrves 4.

Sausage Casserole

1 pound pork sausage 455 g
2 (15 ounce) cans pork
　　and beans　　　　　2 (425 g)
1 (15 ounce) can
　　Mexican stewed
　　tomatoes　　　　　425 g
1 (6 ounce) package
　　corn muffin mix　　170 g
1 egg
⅓ cup milk　　　　　　75 ml

- Preheat oven to 400° (205° C).

- Brown sausage in skillet and drain fat. Add beans and tomatoes, blend and bring to a boil.

- Pour into sprayed 3-quart (3 L) baking dish. Prepare muffin with egg and milk in bowl. Drop teaspoonfuls of mixture over meat-bean mixture.

- Bake for 30 minutes or until top is brown. Serves 6.

Loaded Potatoes

6 large baking potatoes,
  washed
1 (1 pound) bulk pork
  sausage   455 g
1 (8 ounce) package
  cubed Velveeta®
  cheese   230 g
1 (10 ounce) can diced
  tomatoes and green
  chilies   280 g

- Cook potatoes in microwave until done. Brown sausage in skillet over medium heat and drain fat. Add cheese and tomatoes and green chilies and stir well.

- With knife, cut potatoes down center and fluff insides with fork.

- Spoon generous amounts of sausage-cheese mixture on each potato and reheat in microwave for 2 to 3 minutes, if necessary. Serves 6.

Italian Sausage and Ravioli

1 pound sweet Italian
  pork sausage   455 g
1 (26 ounce) jar extra
  chunky mushroom
  and green pepper
  spaghetti sauce   740 g
1 (20 ounce) package
  frozen cheese-filled
  ravioli, cooked,
  drained   570 g
Grated parmesan cheese

- Remove casing from sausage and cook in large skillet over medium heat until brown and no longer pink. Stir to separate sausage and drain. Stir in spaghetti sauce and heat to boiling.

- Cook ravioli according to package directions and add to spaghetti and sausage. Sprinkle with parmesan cheese and pour into serving dish. Serves 6 to 8.

Pork-Stuffed Eggplant

1 large eggplant
¾ pound ground pork   340 g
½ pound pork sausage   230 g
1 egg
½ cup seasoned
   breadcrumbs   60 g
½ cup grated romano
   cheese   50 g
1 tablespoon dried
   parsley flakes   15 ml
1 tablespoon dried onion
   flakes   15 ml
1 teaspoon dried oregano   5 ml
1 (15 ounce) can stewed
   tomatoes   425 g
1 (8 ounce) can tomato
   sauce   230 g

- Preheat oven to 350° (175° C).

- Cut off eggplant stem and cut in half lengthwise. Scoop out and reserve center, leaving a ½-inch (1.2 cm) shell.

- Steam shell halves for about 5 minutes or just until tender. Drain well. Cube reserved eggplant and cook in saucepan with boiling salt water for about 6 minutes, drain well and set aside.

- Cook pork and sausage in skillet over medium heat until no longer pink and drain. Add eggplant, egg, breadcrumbs, cheese, parsley flakes, onion flakes, oregano, about ½ teaspoon (2 ml) each of salt and pepper and mix well.

- Fill shells and place in sprayed 7 x 11-inch (18 x 28 cm) baking dish. Pour stewed tomatoes and tomato sauce over eggplant. Cover and bake for 30 minutes. Serves 6.

Sausage and Beans

1 (1 pound) fully cooked
    smoked, link sausage   455 g
2 (15 ounce) cans baked
    beans   2 (425 g)
1 (15 ounce) can great
    northern beans,
    drained   425 g
1 (15 ounce) can pinto
    beans, drained   425 g
½ cup chili sauce   135 g
⅔ cup packed brown
    sugar   150 g
1 tablespoon
    Worcestershire sauce 15 ml

- Cut link sausage into 1-inch (2.5 cm) slices. Layer sausage and beans in slow cooker.

- Combine chili sauce, brown sugar, a little black pepper and Worcestershire sauce in bowl and pour over beans and sausage.

- Cover and cook in slow cooker on LOW for 4 hours. Stir before serving. Serves 8.

You can buy sausage in several forms: fresh or cured, cooked, uncooked and dried. Read the labels carefully for cooking instructions.

Zesty Ziti

1 pound Italian sausage
    links, cut into ½-inch
    (1.2 cm) chunks   455 g
1 onion, cut into long
    strips
1 green bell pepper,
    seeded, julienned
1 tablespoon canola oil   15 ml
1 (15 ounce) can diced
    tomatoes   425 g
1 (15 ounce) can Italian
    stewed tomatoes   425 g
2 tablespoons ketchup   35 g
1 (16 ounce) package
    ziti pasta   455 g
1 cup shredded
    mozzarella cheese   115 g

- Preheat oven to 350° (175° C).

- Cook sausage, onion and bell pepper in oil in large skillet over medium heat and drain. Add diced tomatoes, stewed tomatoes and ketchup and mix well.

- Cook ziti according to package directions and drain. Combine sausage-onion mixture and tomato mixture in large bowl and toss with pasta and cheese. Spoon into sprayed 3-quart (3 L) baking dish. Cover and bake for 20 minutes. Serves 8.

Pizza Pies

½ **pound bulk turkey**
    sausage   **230 g**
⅔ **cup pizza sauce**   **170 g**
1 **(10 ounce) package**
    refrigerated pizza
    dough   **280 g**
½ **cup shredded**
    mozzarella cheese   **60 g**

- Preheat oven to 400° (205° C).

- Brown sausage in skillet and stir to break up pieces of meat. Drain fat, add pizza sauce and heat until bubbly.

- Unroll pizza dough, place on flat surface and pat into 8 x 12-inch (20 x 32 cm) rectangle. Cut into 6 squares.

- Divide sausage mixture evenly among squares and sprinkle with cheese. Lift one corner of each square and fold over filling to make triangle.

- Press edges together with tines of fork to seal. Bake for about 12 minutes or until light golden brown. Serve immediately. Serves 6.

TIP: Use this short-cut version of pizza or put your favorite ingredients inside – I like "double cheese" on mine, but check your refrigerator for extras. (Additional ingredients may need to be cooked before adding.)

As-Easy-as-Falling-Off-a-Log Baked Ham

Yes, it really is that easy! The best part is that people will rave about it and want to know your recipe.

1 (4 - 5 pound) shank or butt-portion ham   2 - 2.5 kg

- Preheat oven to 350° (175° C).

- Unwrap plastic wrapping around ham and place in large roasting pan. Wrap foil over top and seal edges around pan opening.

- Bake for 3 to 3 hours 30 minutes. Remove foil, place ham on large platter and slice. Serves 8.

TIP: This isn't the prettiest cut of pork in the grocery store, but it sure is tasty. When you have sliced the meat off the bone, you have great seasoning with the bone and meat scraps.

Easy Baked Chops

4 (½ - 1 inch) pork chops   4 (1.2 cm)
Canola oil
1 - 2 tablespoons onion soup mix   15 - 30 ml
2 tablespoons French salad dressing   30 ml

- Preheat oven to 350° (175° C).

- Brown pork chops on both sides in large skillet with a little oil. Sprinkle soup mix over top.

- Pour in salad dressing and ¼ cup (60 ml) cup water. Cover and bake for about 1 hour. Serves 4.

Seaworthy Seafood

Hooked, Caught and in-the-Pan

Seaworthy Seafood Contents

No-Noodle Tuna

1(8 ounce) tube refrigerated crescent rolls	230 g
1 cup shredded white cheddar cheese	115 g
1 (10 ounce) box frozen chopped broccoli, thawed	280 g
4 eggs, beaten	
1 (2 ounce) box cream of broccoli soup mix	60 g
1 (8 ounce) carton sour cream	230 g
1 cup milk	250 ml
½ cup mayonnaise	110 g
2 tablespoons dried onion flakes	30 ml
½ teaspoon dill weed	2 ml
2 (6 ounce) cans white meat tuna, drained, flaked	2 (170 g)
1 (2 ounce) jar diced pimentos	60 g

- Preheat oven to 350° (175° C).

- Unroll crescent roll dough into one long rectangle and place in 9 x 13-inch (23 x 33 cm) baking dish.

- Seal seams and press on bottom and ½ inch (1.2 cm) up sides. Sprinkle with cheese and chopped broccoli.

- Combine eggs, broccoli soup mix, sour cream, milk, mayonnaise, onion flakes and dill weed in bowl and mix well. Stir in tuna and pimentos. Pour over broccoli-cheese in baking dish.

- Cover and bake for 40 minutes or until knife inserted in center comes out clean. Cut into squares to serve. Serves 8.

Ever-Ready Tuna Casserole

1 (7 ounce) package
  elbow macaroni   200 g
1 (8 ounce) package
  shredded Velveeta®
  cheese   230 g
2 (6 ounce) cans
  tuna, drained   2 (170 g)
1 (10 ounce) can
  cream of celery
  soup   280 g
1 cup milk   250 ml

- Preheat oven to 350° (175° C).

- Cook macaroni according to package directions. Drain well, add cheese and stir until cheese melts.

- Add tuna, celery soup and milk and continue stirring. Spoon into sprayed 7 x 11-inch (18 x 28 cm) baking dish. Cover and bake for 35 minutes or until bubbly. Serves 6.

Tuna-Stuffed Tomatoes

4 large tomatoes
2 (6 ounce) cans
  white meat tuna,
  drained   2 (170 g)
2 cups chopped celery 200 g
½ cup chopped
  cashews   70 g
1 small zucchini with
  peel, finely
  chopped
½ cup mayonnaise   110 g

- Cut thin slice off top of each tomato, scoop out flesh and discard. Turn tomatoes, top down on paper towels to drain.

- Combine tuna, celery, cashews, zucchini, mayonnaise and a little salt and pepper in bowl and mix well. Spoon mixture into hollowed-out tomatoes. Refrigerate. Serves 4.

Tuna-Asparagus Pot Pie

1 (8 ounce) package
   crescent rolls, divided   230 g
1 (6 ounce) can solid
   white tuna in water,
   drained   170 g
1 (15 ounce) can cut
   asparagus, drained   425 g
1 cup shredded cheddar
   cheese   115 g

- Preheat oven to 375° (190° C).

- Form 7-inch (18 cm) square using 4 crescent rolls, pinch edges together to seal and place in sprayed 8 x 8-inch (20 x 20 cm) square baking pan.

- Spread dough with tuna, then asparagus and cheese. Form remaining 4 crescent rolls into 1 square and place on top of cheese.

- Bake for 20 minutes or until top browns and cheese bubbles. Serves 4.

Tubular pastas are hollow tube-like shapes that come in many different lengths and diameters. Common elbow macaroni is an example of "tube" pasta.

Cannaroni	*wide tubes*
Cannelloni	*large tubes used for stuffing*
Ditali	*very short tubes*
Gigantoni	*very large tubes used for stuffing*
Manicotti	*very large tubes used for stuffing*
Mostaccioli	*"little moustaches"; smooth tubes*
Penne	*small tubes cut diagonally*
Rigatoni	*large tubes with ridges on outside*
Tubetti	*very small tubes*

Ever-Ready Sauce for Tuna

Sauce:

1 tablespoon olive oil	15 ml
2 teaspoons minced garlic	10 ml
2 teaspoons sugar	10 ml
¼ teaspoon cayenne pepper	1 ml
2 teaspoons dried basil	10 ml
1 (15 ounce) can stewed tomatoes	425 g

- Heat olive oil in saucepan and add garlic, sugar, cayenne pepper and basil. Cook on low heat for 2 minutes.

- Add stewed tomatoes, bring to a boil, reduce heat and simmer for 20 minutes.

Tuna:

1 (12 ounce) can water-packed tuna, drained	340 g
¾ cup pitted, green olives, sliced	95 g
¼ cup drained capers	30 g
1 cup pasta, cooked	165 g

- Combine tuna, olives, capers and pasta in bowl, stir in sauce and toss. Serves 6.

Pasta needs a lot of water to cook properly. Use at least two quarts for every eight ounces of dried pasta.

Tuna-in-the-Straw

1 (8 ounce) package
   egg noodles   230 g
2 (10 ounce) cans
   cream of chicken
   soup   2 (280 g)
1 (8 ounce) carton
   sour cream   230 g
1 teaspoon Creole
   seasoning   5 ml
½ cup milk   125 ml
2 (6 ounce) cans white
   meat tuna,
   drained, flaked   2 (170 g)
1 cup shredded
   Velveeta® cheese 115 g
1 (10 ounce) box
   green peas,
   thawed   280 g
1 (2 ounce) jar diced
   pimento   60 g
1 (1.5 ounce) can
   shoe-string
   potatoes   45 g

- Preheat oven to 350° (175° C).

- Cook noodles according to package directions and drain. Combine soup, sour cream, Creole seasoning and milk in large saucepan and mix well.

- Add noodles, tuna, cheese, peas and pimento to saucepan. Pour into sprayed 9 x 13-inch (23 x 33 cm) baking dish. Sprinkle shoe-string potatoes on top.

- Bake for about 35 minutes or until shoe-string potatoes are light brown. Serves 6.

Alfredo Salmon and Noodles

3 cups medium egg noodles	285 g
1 (16 ounce) package frozen broccoli florets, thawed	455 g
1 cup alfredo sauce	270 g
1 (15 ounce) can salmon, drained, boned	425 g

- Cook noodles in large saucepan according to package directions. Add broccoli last 5 minutes of cooking time and drain. (Discard broccoli stems.)

- Stir in alfredo sauce and salmon and cook on low heat, stirring occasionally, until mixture heats through. Pour into serving bowl. Serves 6.

TIP: *You can make the alfredo sauce yourself, buy it fresh in the refrigerated section of the grocery store or buy it in a jar. The time is up to you.*

Pan-Fried Flounder

1 tablespoon plus 1 teaspoon seafood seasoning, divided	20 ml
¼ teaspoon cayenne pepper	1 ml
⅔ cup flour	980 g
¼ cup olive oil	60 ml
6 - 8 small flounder fillets	
¾ cup tartar sauce	170 g
⅓ cup ketchup	90 g

- Combine 1 tablespoon (15 ml) seafood seasoning, cayenne pepper, flour, ¼ teaspoon (1 ml) pepper and ½ teaspoon (2 ml) salt in bowl.

- Heat oil over high heat in large skillet. Dredge each fillet in flour-seasoning mixture and place in skillet (in batches). Fry for about 3 minutes on each side, depending on thickness of fillets. Drain on paper towels.

- Combine tartar sauce, ketchup and 1 teaspoon (5 ml) seafood seasoning in bowl and serve with fried flounder. Serves 6.

Sunday Best Fried Fish

1 (16 ounce) package cooked, frozen batter-dipped fish	455 g
1 cup spaghetti sauce	250 g
2 teaspoons Italian seasoning	10 ml
1 cup shredded mozzarella cheese	115 g

- Heat fish according to package directions. While fish is heating, combine spaghetti sauce and Italian seasoning in bowl.

- When fish heats thoroughly, place each piece on serving plate and spoon spaghetti mixture over fish. Sprinkle cheese on top and serve. Serve 6.

Broiled Red Snapper

2 tablespoons dijon-style mustard	30 ml
¼ cup Italian salad dressing	60 ml
4 (6 ounce) red snapper fillets	4 (170 g)

- Preheat broiler. Combine mustard and Italian dressing in small bowl.

- Place snapper, skin-side down on sprayed, foil-lined baking pan.

- Brush mustard-dressing mixture over fillets and broil for about 8 minutes or until snapper flakes easily when tested with fork. Serves 4.

Grilled Swordfish with Pepper Sauce

4 (1 inch) swordfish
   steaks   4 (2.5 cm)
3 tablespoons olive oil 45 ml
¾ teaspoon seasoned
   salt   4 ml
½ teaspoon lemon
   pepper   2 ml

- Rub swordfish with olive oil and sprinkle with seasoned salt and lemon pepper.

- Grill over medium-high heat for about 10 minutes, turning once or until it cooks thoroughly. (Do not overcook. It will dry fish out.)

Sauce:

⅓ cup roasted red pepper 80 ml
1 tablespoon dijon-style
   mustard   15 ml
3 tablespoons mayonnaise 35 g

- Place all sauce ingredients and ½ teaspoon (2 ml) pepper in blender and process until they blend well. Serve over grilled swordfish. Serves 4.

The most important thing to remember about cooking fish is not to overcook it. The internal temperature should be about 145° and the flesh should be opaque. Don't let fish dry out.

Extra Special Fried Fish

1 (16 ounce) package cooked,
   frozen batter-dipped
   fried fish   455 g
¾ cup chili sauce   205 g
1 bunch fresh green
   onions, chopped
1 cup shredded cheddar
   cheese   115 g

- Preheat oven to 325° (160° C).

- Arrange fish in sprayed 9 x 13-inch (23 x 33 cm) glass baking dish and heat for about 20 minutes or just until fish heats thoroughly.

- Heat chili sauce in saucepan and spoon over each piece of fish. Top with green onions and cheddar cheese. Serve right from baking dish. Serves 6.

Skillet Shrimp Scampi

2 teaspoons olive oil   10 ml
2 pounds shrimp, peeled,
   veined   200 g
⅔ cup herb-garlic
   marinade with lemon
   juice   150 ml
¼ cup finely chopped
   green onion with tops 25 g
Rice or pasta, cooked

- Heat oil in large non-stick skillet. Add shrimp and marinade and cook, stirring often, until shrimp turn pink.

- Stir in green onions. Serve over rice or pasta. Serves 6.

Red Snapper with Fresh Salsa

6 (6 ounce) red
  snapper fillets   6 (170 g)
Canola oil
1 teaspoon ground
  cumin   5 ml
½ teaspoon cayenne
  pepper   2 ml

- Dry snapper with paper towels and rub a little oil on both sides of snapper. Sprinkle with cumin, cayenne pepper and ½ teaspoon (2 ml) salt.

- Grill snapper for about 5 minutes on each side or until fish flakes easily when tested with fork.

Salsa:

½ cup chopped fresh
  cilantro   10 g
1 (15 ounce) can great
  northern beans,
  drained   425 g
1 (15 ounce) can Italian
  stewed tomatoes,
  drained   425 g
⅓ cup chopped green
  olives   45 g
1 teaspoon minced garlic 5 ml

- Combine cilantro, beans, tomatoes, olives and garlic in bowl and mix well. Serve with each red snapper and garnish with slice of fresh lime, if you like. Serves 6.

Salmon and Green Beans

Canola oil
4 (6 ounce) salmon steaks   4 (170 g)
¼ cup lite soy sauce   60 ml
2 tablespoon lemon juice   30 ml
1 (10 ounce) package frozen whole green beans   280 g
Rice, cooked

- Place a little oil in skillet over medium-high heat and add salmon steaks. Combine soy sauce and lemon juice in bowl and pour over steaks.

- Cover and cook for about 5 minutes. Turn salmon and place green beans over salmon with 2 tablespoons (30 ml) water.

- Cover and steam for 5 minutes or until beans are tender-crisp. Season green beans with a little salt and pepper and serve over rice. Serves 4.

Even with the high content of fats in the Chinook salmon, all salmon are rated highly for their protein, B-group vitamins, vitamin A and Omega-3 oils.

Salmon Casserole

1 (6 ounce) package
    dried egg noodles   170 g
1 (10 ounce) can cream
    of celery soup   280 g
1 (5 ounce) can
    evaporated milk   145 g
1 tablespoon lemon juice   15 ml
½ onion, chopped
1 (15 ounce) can salmon,
    skin removed, boned   425 g
1 cup shredded cheddar
    cheese   240 ml
1 (8 ounce) can small
    green peas, drained   230 g
½ teaspoon seasoned salt   2 ml
¼ teaspoon white pepper   1 ml
½ teaspoon Creole
    seasoning   2 ml
1 cup crushed cheese
    crackers   60 g
2 tablespoons butter,
    melted   30 g

- Preheat oven to 350° (175° C).

- Cook noodles according to package directions and drain.

- Stir in soup, evaporated milk, lemon juice, onion, salmon, cheese, peas, seasoned salt, white pepper and Creole seasoning. Spoon into sprayed 7 x 11-inch (18 x 28 cm) baking dish. Cover and bake for 25 minutes.

- Combine cheese crackers and butter in bowl and sprinkle over casserole. Return to oven for 10 minutes or until crumbs are light brown. Serves 8.

Thai Shrimp-Peanut Noodles

1 (5.5 ounce) box Thai
    stir-fry rice noodles
    with seasoning packet 155 g
1 pound peeled, veined
    shrimp   455 g
1 (10 ounce) package
    frozen broccoli
    florets, thawed   280 g
Canola oil
½ cup peanuts   73 g

- Boil 3 cups (750 ml) water in saucepan and stir in noodles. Turn heat off and soak noodles for about 5 minutes. Drain and rinse in cold water.

- Saute shrimp and broccoli in skillet with a little oil for about 8 minutes or just until shrimp turns pink.

- Add softened noodles, seasoning packet and peanuts. (There are chopped peanuts in seasoning, but this dish is better, if you add more peanuts.) Serves 6.

TIP: If noodles are still too firm after they soak, add 1 tablespoon (15 ml) water and stir-fry until noodles are tender.

Shrimp is available in hundreds of varieties, but they can generally be divided between warm-water shrimp and cold-water shrimp. As a general rule, cold-water shrimp are smaller, but more succulent. All varieties range in colors from deep red, pink, white, gray and green. Most change color when cooked.

Savory Shrimp Fettuccini

2 tablespoons butter	30 g
⅓ cup chopped onion	55 g
1 teaspoon seafood seasoning	5 ml
½ pound small shrimp, peeled, veined	230 g
1 (10 ounce) can cream of shrimp soup	280 g
½ cup half-and-half cream	155 g
½ cup mayonnaise	110 g
2 teaspoons white wine Worcestershire sauce	10 ml
½ teaspoon horseradish	2 ml
1 cup shredded white cheddar cheese, divided	115 g
1 (8 ounce) package fettuccini, cooked	230 g
1 (16 ounce) package frozen broccoli florets, cooked	455 g

- Preheat oven to 350° (175° C).

- In large saucepan, melt butter in large saucepan and saute onion. Add seafood seasoning and shrimp and cook, while stirring until shrimp turn pink, about 2 minutes.

- Add shrimp soup, half-and-half cream, mayonnaise, Worcestershire, horseradish and half cheese. Heat just until cheese melts. Fold in fettuccini.

- When broccoli cools from cooking, cut some stems away and discard. Fold broccoli into sauce.

- Spoon into sprayed 3-quart (3 L) baking dish. Cover and bake for 30 minutes.

- Remove from oven and sprinkle remaining cheese on top and bake for additional 5 minutes. Serves 8.

Fettuccini of the Sea

¼ cup (½ stick) butter	60 g
¼ cup flour	30 g
1 teaspoon Creole seasoning	5 ml
¾ teaspoon white pepper	4 ml
1 tablespoon minced garlic	15 ml
1 (16 ounce) carton half-and-half cream	455 g
½ cup milk	125 ml
½ cup finely chopped red bell pepper	75 g
2 (6 ounce) cans tiny shrimp, veined	2 (170 g)
2 (6 ounce) cans crabmeat, picked, drained	2 (170 g)
1 (6 ounce) can chopped clams, drained	170 g
½ cup grated parmesan cheese	50 g
1 (12 ounce) package fettuccini, cooked al dente	340 g
Parsley	

- Preheat oven to 325° (160° C).

- Melt butter in saucepan and add flour, Creole seasoning, white pepper and garlic and mix well. On medium heat, gradually add half-and-half cream and milk and mix well. Cook, stirring constantly until it thickens.

- Add bell pepper, shrimp, crabmeat, clams and parmesan cheese and heat thoroughly. Spoon half fettuccini and half seafood sauce into sprayed 9 x 13-inch (23 x 33 cm) baking dish. Repeat layers.

- Cover and bake for 25 minutes or just until casserole is bubbly. To serve, sprinkle parsley over top of casserole. Serves 8.

Crab-Stuffed Baked Potatoes

This potato is truly a meal in itself!

4 large baking potatoes
½ cup (1 stick) butter 115 g
½ cup whipping
** cream   40 g**
1 bunch fresh green
** onions, chopped**
2 (6 ounce) cans
** crabmeat,**
** drained, flaked   2 (170 g)**
¾ cup shredded
** cheddar cheese   85 g**
2 tablespoons fresh
** minced parsley   30 ml**

- Preheat oven to 375° (190° C).

- Bake potatoes for 1 hour or until well done. Halve each potato lengthwise and scoop out flesh, but leave skins intact.

- Mash potatoes with butter in large bowl. Add whipping cream, ¾ teaspoon (4 ml) salt, ½ teaspoon (2 ml) pepper and green onions. Stir in crabmeat.

- Fill reserved potato skins with potato mixture. Sprinkle with cheese. Bake at 350° (175° C) for about 15 minutes. To serve, sprinkle fresh parsley over cheese. Serves 4.

Russet potatoes are used for baking and are also called baking potatoes or Idaho potatoes. The starch content make these excellent for baking, frying and boiling.

No-Panic Crab Casserole

2 (6 ounce) cans
  crabmeat, drained,
  flaked   2 (170 g)
1 cup half-and-half
  cream   155 g
1½ cups mayonnaise   335 g
6 eggs, hard-boiled,
  finely chopped
1 cup seasoned
  breadcrumbs,
  divided   120 g
1 tablespoon dried
  parsley flakes   15 ml
½ teaspoon dried
  basil   2 ml
1 (8 ounce) can sliced
  water chestnuts,
  drained   230 g
2 tablespoons butter,
  melted   30 g

- Preheat oven to 350° (175° C).

- Combine crabmeat, half-and-half cream, mayonnaise, eggs, ½ cup (60 g) seasoned breadcrumbs, parsley, basil, water chestnuts and a little salt and pepper in bowl and mix well.

- Pour into sprayed 2-quart (2 L) baking dish.

- Combine remaining breadcrumbs and butter and sprinkle over top of casserole.

- Bake for 40 minutes. Serve 6.

Creamed Shrimp over Rice

3 (10 ounce) cans
   cream of shrimp
   soup   3 (280 g)
1 pint sour cream   455 g
1½ teaspoons curry
   powder   7 ml
2 (6 ounce) cans
   veined shrimp 2 (170 g)
Rice, cooked

- Combine all ingredients in double boiler. Heat and stir constantly but do not boil.

- Serve over rice. Serves 4.

Shrimp Newburg

1 (10 ounce) can cream
   of shrimp soup   280 g
1 teaspoon seafood
   seasoning   5 ml
1 (1 pound) package
   cooked, frozen salad
   shrimp, thawed 455 g
Rice, cooked

- Combine soup, ¼ cup (60 ml) water and seafood seasoning in saucepan. Bring to a boil, reduce heat and stir in shrimp.

- Heat thoroughly and serve over rice. Serves 6.

Shrimp Quantities per Pound

Prawns (colossal)	10 or less per pound
Prawns (jumbo)	11-15 per pound
Extra Large	16-20 per pound
Large	21-30 per pound
Medium	31-35 per pound
Small	36-45 per pound
Miniature	100 per pound

Shrimp in Sour Cream

2 green onions, chopped
8 ounces fresh
   mushrooms, washed,
   drained, sliced   230 g
2 tablespoons butter   30 g
1 pound (18 - 22 count)
   shrimp, cooked,
   peeled, cleaned   455 g
1 tablespoon flour   15 ml
1 teaspoon Worcestershire
   sauce   5 ml
2 tablespoons dry sherry   30 ml
1 (8 ounce) carton sour
   cream   230 g
Rice, cooked

- Saute green onions and mushrooms in butter in skillet for 5 minutes.

- Add shrimp and heat. Sprinkle mixture with flour, Worcestershire, ½ teaspoon (2 ml) each of salt and pepper. Add sherry and sour cream, mix well.

- Cook over low heat until hot, but do not let boil. Serve over rice. Serves 8.

Shrimp is America's favorite shellfish and comes mostly from the Pacific and Atlantic Oceans and the Gulf of Mexico. In general 1 pound of uncooked shrimp will yield about ¾ pound cooked shrimp

Shrimp Scampi

½ cup (1 stick) butter   115 g
3 cloves garlic, pressed
¼ cup lemon juice   60 ml
Hot sauce
2 pounds shrimp, peeled   910 g

- Melt butter in skillet, saute garlic and add lemon juice and a few dashes of hot sauce.

- Arrange shrimp in single layer in shallow pan. Pour garlic-butter over shrimp and salt lightly.

- Broil for 2 minutes, turn shrimp and broil for additional 2 minutes. Reserve garlic butter and serve separately. Serves 6.

Orange Roughy with Peppers

1 pound orange roughy
    fillets   455 g
1 onion, sliced
2 red bell peppers,
    julienned
1 teaspoon dried thyme
    leaves   5 ml
¼ teaspoon black pepper   1 ml

- Cut fish into 4 serving-size pieces. Heat a little oil in skillet. Layer onion and bell peppers and sprinkle with half thyme and pepper.

- Place fish over peppers and sprinkle with remaining thyme and pepper.

- Turn burner on high until fish is hot enough to cook. Lower heat, cover and cook fish for 15 to 20 minutes or until fish flakes easily. Serves 6.

Neptune Lasagna

3 tablespoons butter	45 g
1 red bell pepper, chopped	
1 onion, chopped	
1 (8 ounce) package cream cheese, softened	230 g
1½ cups small curd cottage cheese	340 g
1 egg, beaten	
2 teaspoons dried basil	10 ml
2 teaspoons Creole seasoning	10 ml
1 (10 ounce) can cream of shrimp soup	280 g
1 (10 ounce) can cream of celery soup	280 g
½ cup white wine	125 ml
¾ cup milk	175 ml
2 (8 ounce) packages imitation crabmeat	2 (230 g)
1 (8 ounce) package salad shrimp, rinsed, drained	230 g
9 lasagna noodles, cooked, drained	
⅓ cup grated parmesan cheese	35 g
1 cup shredded white cheddar cheese	115 g

- Preheat oven to 350° (175° C).

- Heat butter in skillet and saute bell pepper and onion. Reduce heat and add cream cheese and stir until cream cheese melts. Remove from heat and add cottage cheese, egg, 2 teaspoons (10 ml) basil, ½ teaspoon (2 ml) pepper and Creole seasoning and set aside.

- Combine soups, white wine, milk, crabmeat and shrimp in bowl and mix well.

- Arrange 3 noodles in sprayed 9 x 13-inch (23 x 33 cm) baking dish. Spread with one-third of cottage cheese mixture and one-third seafood mixture. Repeat layers twice. Sprinkle with parmesan cheese.

- Cover and bake for about 40 minutes.

- Uncover and sprinkle with white cheddar cheese and bake for additional 10 minutes or until casserole bubbles. Let stand for at least 15 minutes before serving. Serves 8 to 10.

No Ordinary Shrimp

½ cup chopped onion	160 g
1 red bell pepper, thinly sliced	
5 tablespoons butter, divided	75 g
2 tablespoons flour	15 g
¾ cup half-and-half cream	235 g
1 teaspoon marinade for chicken (Lea & Perrins)	5 ml
3 cups cooked, peeled, veined shrimp	420 g
2 cups cooked white rice	560 g
¾ cup shredded cheddar cheese	85 g
¾ cup round buttery cracker crumbs	45 g

- Preheat oven to 350° (175° C).

- Saute onion and bell pepper in 3 tablespoons (45 g) butter in skillet, but do not brown.

- Blend in flour, ½ teaspoon (2 ml) each of salt and pepper, heat and mix well.

- On medium heat, gradually add half-and-half cream and Worcestershire and stir until it thickens. Fold in shrimp.

- Place cooked rice in sprayed 7 x 11-inch (18 x 28 cm) baking dish and spread out. Pour shrimp mixture over rice.

- Sprinkle cheese over top and combine cracker crumbs and remaining melted butter in bowl. Sprinkle over casserole.

- Bake for about 20 to 25 minutes or until crumbs are light brown. Served 8.

BONUS!
Desserts

Cold, Hot,
Creamy, Crispy
and Yummy

BONUS! Desserts Contents

Sweet Angel Cake

This gets rave reviews whenever we serve it. It's one of our favorites.

1½ cups powdered sugar	180 g
⅓ cup milk	75 ml
1 (8 ounce) package cream cheese, softened	230 g
1 (3.5 ounce) can flaked coconut	100 g
1 cup chopped pecans	110 g
1 (12 ounce) carton whipped topping, thawed	340 g
1 large angel food cake, torn into bite-size pieces	
1 (16 ounce) can cherry pie filling	455 g

- Add powdered sugar and milk to cream cheese and beat in bowl.

- Fold in coconut and pecans, stir in whipped topping and cake pieces.

- Spread in 9 x 13-inch (23 x 33 cm) glass dish and refrigerate for several hours.

- Add pie filling by tablespoon on top of cake mixture. (It will not cover cake mixture, but it will just be in clumps, making a pretty red and white dessert.)

- Refrigerate. Serves 15 to 16.

Colored Sugar

You can easily make your own colored sugar to use on cookies and cakes by adding a few drops of food color and mixing well until all the sugar is coated. Add 2 drops to ¼ cup sugar.

Chocolate Hurricane Cake

This is easy and very, very yummy.

1 cup chopped pecans	110 g
1 (3 ounce) can sweetened flaked coconut	85 g
1 (18 ounce) box German chocolate cake mix	510 g
⅓ cup canola oil	75 ml
3 eggs	
½ cup (1 stick) butter, melted	115 g
1 (8 ounce) package cream cheese, softened	230 g
1 (16 ounce) box powdered sugar	455 g

- Preheat oven to 350° (175° C).

- Cover bottom of sprayed, floured 9 x 13-inch (23 x 33 cm) baking pan with pecans and coconut.

- Combine cake mix, 1¼ cups (310 ml) water, oil and eggs in bowl and beat well. Carefully pour batter over pecans and coconut.

- Combine butter, cream cheese and powdered sugar in bowl and whip to blend. Spoon mixture over unbaked batter and bake for 40 to 42 minutes. Serves 18.

TIP: You cannot test for doneness with toothpick because this cake will appear sticky even when it is done. The frosting sinks into bottom as it bakes and forms white ribbon inside.

Turtle Cake WOW!

1 (18 ounce) box German chocolate cake mix	510 g
½ cup (1 stick) butter, softened	115 g
½ cup canola oil	125 ml
1 (14 ounce) can sweetened condensed milk, divided	400 g
1 (1 pound) bag caramels	455 g
1 cup chopped pecans	110 g

- Preheat oven to 350° (175° C).

- Combine cake mix, butter, 1½ cups (375 ml) water, oil and half sweetened condensed milk. Pour half batter into sprayed, floured 9 x 13-inch (23 x 33 cm) baking pan and bake for 20 minutes.

- Melt caramels and blend with remaining sweetened condensed milk. Spread evenly over baked cake layer and sprinkle with pecans. Cover with remaining batter and bake for an additional 20 to 25 minutes.

Frosting:

½ cup (1 stick) butter	115 g
3 tablespoons cocoa	15 g
6 tablespoons evaporated milk	90 ml
1 (16 ounce) box powdered sugar	455 g
1 teaspoon vanilla	5 ml

- Melt butter in saucepan and mix in cocoa and milk. Add powdered sugar and vanilla to mixture and blend well. Spread over cake. Serves 24.

Coconut Cake Deluxe

This cake is really moist and delicious and can be frozen if you need to make it in advance.

1 (18 ounce) box yellow
    cake mix   510 g
1 (14 ounce) can
    sweetened condensed
    milk   400 g
1 (15 ounce) can coconut
    cream   425 g
1 (3 ounce) can flaked
    coconut   85 g
1 (8 ounce) carton
    whipped topping,
    thawed   230 g

- Preheat oven to 350° (175° C).

- Prepare cake mix according to package directions and pour into sprayed, floured 9 x 13-inch (23 x 33 cm) baking pan.

- Bake for 30 to 35 minutes or until toothpick inserted in center comes out clean. While cake is warm, punch holes in cake about 2 inches (5 cm) apart.

- Pour sweetened condensed milk over cake and spread around until all milk soaks into cake. Pour coconut cream over cake and sprinkle coconut on top. Cool and frost with whipped topping. Serves 12 to 15.

Easy Breezy Pineapple Cake

2 cups sugar	400 g
2 cups flour	240 g
1 (20 ounce) can crushed pineapple with juice	570 g
1 teaspoon baking soda	5 ml
1 teaspoon vanilla	5 ml

- Preheat oven to 350° (175° C).

- Combine all cake ingredients and ½ teaspoon (2 ml) salt in bowl and mix well with spoon.

- Pour into sprayed, floured 9 x 13-inch (23 x 33 cm) baking pan and bake for 30 to 35 minutes. Frost while hot.

Frosting:

1 (8 ounce) package cream cheese, softened	230 g
½ cup (1 stick) butter, melted	115 g
1 cup powdered sugar	120 g
1 cup chopped pecans	110 g

- Beat all ingredients except pecans in bowl.

- Add pecans, stir to mix well and spread over hot cake. Serves 12.

Apply frosting with a metal spatula to get a nice smooth finish. (If you're using a frosting that's somewhat thick, you can also dip your spatula in hot water to warm it, then wipe the water off. This will make smoothing the frosting over the cake easier.)

Oreo Cake

1 (18 ounce) box white
   cake mix   510 g
⅓ cup canola oil   75 ml
4 egg whites
1¼ cups coarsely crushed
   Oreo® cookies   75 g

- Preheat oven to 350° (175° C).

- Combine cake mix, 1¼ cups (310 ml) water, oil and egg whites in large bowl. Blend on low speed until moist. Beat for 2 minutes on high speed and gently fold in coarsely crushed cookies.

- Pour batter into 2 sprayed, floured 8 or 9-inch (20 or 23 cm) cake pans and bake for 25 to 30 minutes or until toothpick inserted in center comes out clean. Cool for 10 minutes, remove from pan and cool.

Frosting:

4¼ cups powdered sugar 510 g
1 cup (2 sticks) butter,
   softened   230 g
1 cup shortening (not
   butter flavored)   190 g
1 teaspoon almond
   flavoring   5 ml
¼ cup crushed Oreo®
   cookies   15 g
¼ cup chopped pecans   30 g

- Beat all ingredients except crushed cookie pieces and pecans in bowl. Frost first layer, place second layer on top and frost top and sides. Sprinkle crushed cookies and pecans on top. Serves 20.

TIP: The butter-flavored shortening is not best for this recipe, so use regular unflavored shortening.

Pina Colada Cake

1 (18 ounce) box orange
   cake mix   **510 g**
3 eggs
⅓ cup canola oil   **75 ml**
1 (14 ounce) can
   sweetened condensed
   milk   **400 g**
1 (15 ounce) can coconut
   cream   **425 g**
1 cup flaked coconut   **85 g**
1 (8 ounce) can crushed
   pineapple, drained   **230 g**
1 (8 ounce) carton
   whipped topping,
   thawed   **230 g**

- Preheat oven to 350° (175° C).

- Combine cake mix, eggs, 1¼ cups (310 ml) water and oil in bowl. Beat for 3 or 4 minutes and pour into sprayed, floured 10 x 15-inch (25 x 38 cm) baking pan.

- Bake for 35 minutes. When cake is done, punch holes in cake with fork so frosting will soak into cake.

- Mix sweetened condensed milk, coconut cream, coconut and pineapple in bowl. While cake is warm, pour mixture over cake. Refrigerate until cake is cold, spread layer whipped topping over cake and return to refrigerator. Serves 22.

Chocolate-Cherry Cake

1 (18 ounce) box milk
  chocolate cake mix   510 g
1 (20 ounce) can cherry
  pie filling   570 g
3 eggs

- Preheat oven to 350° (175° C).

- Combine cake mix, pie filling
  and eggs in bowl and mix with
  spoon. Pour into sprayed,
  floured 9 x 13-inch (23 x 33 cm)
  baking dish.

- Bake for 35 to 40 minutes. Cake
  is done when toothpick inserted
  in center comes out clean.

- Spread frosting over hot cake.

Frosting:

5 tablespoons butter   75 g
1¼ cups sugar   250 g
½ cup milk   125 ml
1 (6 ounce) package
  chocolate chips   170 g

- When cake is almost done,
  combine butter, sugar and milk
  in medium saucepan. Boil
  1 minute, stirring constantly.
  Add chocolate chips and stir
  until chips melt. Pour over hot
  cake. Serves 20.

Semi-sweet and sweet chocolate, which comes in baking chips, bars or squares, contains between 15 and 35% chocolate liquor plus sugar and vanilla.

Hawaiian Dream Cake

1 (18 ounce) box yellow cake mix	510 g
4 eggs	
¾ cup canola oil	180 ml
½ (20 ounce) can crushed pineapple with juice	½ (570 g)

- Preheat oven to 350° (175° C).

- Drain pineapple and set aside half of pineapple and half of juice for frosting.

- Beat all ingredients and remaining pineapple and juice in bowl for 4 minutes.

- Pour into sprayed, floured 9 x 13-inch (23 x 33 cm) baking pan.

- Bake for 30 to 35 minutes or until toothpick inserted in center comes out clean. Cool and pour frosting over cake.

Frosting:

½ (20 ounce) can crushed pineapple with juice	½ (570 g)
½ cup (1 stick) butter	115 g
1 (16 ounce) box powdered sugar	455 g
1 (6 ounce) can flaked coconut	170 g

- Heat pineapple and butter in saucepan and boil for 2 minutes.

- Add powdered sugar and coconut.

- Punch holes in cake with knife and pour hot frosting over cake. Serves 20.

Pecan Pie

2 tablespoons flour	15 g
3 tablespoons butter, melted	35 g
3 eggs, beaten	
⅔ cup sugar	135 g
1 cup corn syrup	250 ml
1 teaspoon vanilla	5 ml
1 cup chopped pecans	110 g
1 (9 inch) piecrust	23 cm

- Preheat oven to 350° (175° C).

- Combine flour, butter, eggs, sugar, corn syrup and vanilla in bowl and mix well.

- Place pecans in piecrust and pour egg mixture over pecans.

- Bake for 10 minutes, reduce heat to 275° (140° C) and bake for 50 to 55 minutes or until center of pie is fairly firm. Serves 8.

TIP: Recipe ingredient variations include using 2 tablespoons (30 ml) amaretto liqueur instead of vanilla. Also you could add 1 teaspoon (5 ml) ground cinnamon and ½ teaspoon (2 ml) ground nutmeg.

Creamy Lemon Pie

1 (8 ounce) package cream cheese, softened	230 g
1 (14 ounce) can sweetened condensed milk	400 g
¼ cup lemon juice	60 ml
1 (20 ounce) can lemon pie filling	570 g
1 (6 ounce) ready graham cracker piecrust	170 g

- Beat cream cheese in bowl until smooth and creamy. Add sweetened condensed milk and lemon juice and beat until mixture is creamy.

- Fold in lemon pie filling and stir until mixture blends well. Pour into piecrust and refrigerate for several hours before slicing and serving. Serves 8.

Kahlua Pie

26 **marshmallows**
1 **(12 ounce) can**
    evaporated milk   **340 g**
1 **(1 ounce) package**
    unflavored gelatin   **30 g**
1 **(8 ounce) carton**
    whipping cream   **230 g**
½ **cup Kahlua®**   **125 ml**
1 **(6 ounce) ready**
    chocolate cookie
    piecrust   **170 g**
Chocolate curls

- Melt marshmallows with evaporated milk in saucepan over medium-low heat. Stir constantly and do not let milk boil.

- Dissolve gelatin in ¼ cup (60 ml) cold water. Remove marshmallows mixture from heat and add dissolved gelatin. Refrigerate until mixture thickens slightly.

- Whip cream and fold into marshmallow mixture. Mix in Kahlua® and pour into piecrust. Garnish with chocolate curls and refrigerate overnight. Serves 8.

Why are pie pans round? Colonial housewives literally cut corners to stretch the ingredients. This is also why pie pans are shallow.

Dream Pie

1 (8 ounce) package
   cream cheese,
   softened   230 g
1 (14 ounce) can
   sweetened
   condensed milk   400 g
1 (5 ounce) package
   vanilla instant
   pudding mix   145 g
1 (8 ounce) carton
   whipped topping,
   thawed   230 g
2 (6 ounce) ready
   graham cracker
   ready piecrusts 2 (170 g)
1 (20 ounce) can
   strawberry
   pie filling   570 g

- Beat cream cheese and sweetened condensed milk in bowl until smooth.

- Add pudding mix and ½ cup (125 ml) water, mix and refrigerate for 15 minutes.

- Fold in whipped topping, pour into 2 piecrusts and freeze.

- When ready to serve, remove from freezer and place in refrigerator for 45 minutes before slicing and serving.

- Spoon about ¼ cup (65 g) pie filling on each slice of pie. Serves 16.

TIP: Substitute 2 chocolate ready piecrusts and/or other pie filling flavors. Pour 2 or 3 tablespoons (20 to 25 ml) chocolate ice cream topping over pie and top with chocolate shavings.

Peach-Mousse Pie

1 (16 ounce) package frozen peach slices, thawed	455 g
1 cup sugar	200 g
1 (1 ounce) package unflavored gelatin	30 g
⅛ teaspoon ground nutmeg	.5 ml
A few drops yellow food coloring	
A few drops red food coloring	
1 (12 ounce) carton whipped topping, thawed	340 g
1 (6 ounce) ready graham cracker piecrust	170 g

- Place peaches in blender and process until peaches are smooth. Pour into saucepan, bring to a boil and stir constantly. Remove from heat.

- Combine sugar, gelatin and nutmeg in bowl and stir into hot puree until sugar and gelatin dissolve. Pour gelatin mixture into large bowl and place in freezer for 20 minutes or until mixture mounds. Stir occasionally.

- Beat gelatin mixture on high speed for 5 minutes or until light and fluffy. Add coloring, fold in whipped topping and pour into piecrust. Serves 8.

Outta-Sight Pie

1 (14 ounce) can
   sweetened
   condensed milk   400 g
1 (20 ounce) can
   lemon pie filling   570 g
1 (20 ounce) can
   crushed pineapple,
   drained   570 g
1 (8 ounce) carton
   whipped topping,
   thawed   230 g
2 (6 ounce) ready
   cookie-flavored
   piecrusts   2 (170 g)

- Combine sweetened condensed milk, lemon pie filling and pineapple in saucepan over medium-low heat and mix well.

- Fold in whipped topping and pour mixture into 2 piecrusts. Refrigerate for several hours before serving. Serves 16.

Sweet Potato Pie

1 (15 ounce) can sweet
   potatoes   425 g
¾ cup milk   175 ml
1 cup packed brown
   sugar   220 g
2 eggs
½ teaspoon ground
   cinnamon   2 ml
1 (9 inch) piecrust   23 cm

- Preheat oven to 350° (175° C).

- Combine all ingredients plus ½ teaspoon (2 ml) salt in bowl and blend until smooth.

- Pour into piecrust.

- Bake for 40 minutes or until knife inserted in center comes out clean. (Shield edges of pastry with aluminum foil to prevent excessive browning.) Serves 6.

Apricot Cobbler

A bridge partner served this recently and everybody gave it a blue ribbon. This is another one of those recipes that is really quick and easy plus really delicious.

1 (20 ounce) can apricot pie filling	570 g
1 (20 ounce) can crushed pineapple with juice	570 g
1 cup chopped pecans	110 g
1 (18 ounce) box yellow cake mix	510 g
1 cup (2 sticks) butter, melted	230 g
Whipped topping, thawed	

- Preheat oven to 375° (175° C).

- Pour apricot pie filling into sprayed, floured 9 x 13-inch (23 x 33 cm) baking pan and spread evenly.

- Spoon crushed pineapple and juice over pie filling. Sprinkle pecans over pineapple, then sprinkle cake mix over pecans.

- Pour butter over cake mix and bake for 40 minutes or until light brown and crunchy. To serve, top with whipped topping. Serves 10.

Pecans contain no cholesterol and add essential fiber, vitamin E, magnesium, thiamin and copper to the diet. They are also high in monounsaturated fats that help lower LDL cholesterol levels.

Seven-Layer Cookies

½ cup (1 stick) butter	115 g
1 cup crushed graham crackers	105 g
1 (6 ounce) package semi-sweet chocolate bits	170 g
1 (6 ounce) package butterscotch bits	170 g
1 (3 ounce) can flaked coconut	85 g
1 (14 ounce) can sweetened condensed milk	400 g
1 cup chopped pecans	110 g

• Preheat oven to 350° (175° C).

• Melt butter in 9 x 13-inch (23 x 33 cm) baking pan. Sprinkle remaining ingredients in order listed.

• Do not stir or mix and bake for 30 minutes. Cool before cutting. Serves 15.

Vanishing Butter Cookies

1 (18 ounce) box butter cake mix	510 g
1 (3.4 ounce) package butterscotch instant pudding mix	100 g
1 cup canola oil	250 ml
1 egg, beaten	
1¼ cups chopped pecans	165 g

• Preheat oven to 350° (175° C).

• Mix cake and pudding mixes in bowl with spoon and stir in oil. Add egg, mix thoroughly and stir in pecans.

• Place teaspoonfuls of dough on cookie sheet about 2 inches (5 cm) apart.

• Bake for 8 or 9 minutes. Do not overcook. Yields 3 dozen.

Easy Blonde Brownies

This is another one of those recipes that seems too easy to be a recipe – and you already have everything right in the pantry. These brownies are so good and chewy.

1 (16 ounce) box light brown sugar	455 g
4 eggs	
2 cups biscuit mix	240 g
2 cups chopped pecans	220 g

- Preheat oven to 350° (175° C).

- Beat brown sugar, eggs and biscuit mix in bowl. Stir in pecans.

- Pour into sprayed 9 x 13-inch (23 x 33 cm) baking pan. Bake for 35 minutes. Cool and cut into squares. Serves 20.

Snappy Treats

3 cups quick-cooking oats	240 g
1 cup chocolate chips	170 g
½ cup flaked coconut	85 g
½ cup chopped pecans	110 g
2 cups sugar	400 g
¾ cup (1½ sticks) butter	170 g
½ cup evaporated milk	125 ml

- Combine oats, chocolate chips, coconut and pecans in large bowl.

- Boil sugar, butter and milk in saucepan for 1 to 2 minutes and stir constantly.

- Pour hot mixture over oat-chocolate mixture in bowl and stir until chocolate chips melt.

- Drop teaspoonfuls of mixture onto wax paper. Cool at room temperature and store in covered container. Yields 3 dozen.

TIP: Use white chocolate chips and ¾ cup (130 g) candied, cut-up cherries for a colorful variation.

Buttery Walnut Squares

1 cup (2 sticks) butter,
   softened   230 g
1¾ cups packed brown
   sugar   385 g
1¾ cups flour   180 g

- Preheat oven to 350° (175° C). Combine butter and brown sugar in bowl and beat until smooth and creamy. Add flour and mix well.

- Pat mixture down evenly in sprayed 9 x 13-inch (23 x 33 cm) glass pan and bake for 15 minutes.

Topping:

1 cup packed brown
   sugar   220 g
4 eggs, lightly beaten
2 tablespoons flour   15 g
2 cups chopped walnuts 260 g
1 cup flaked coconut   85 g

- Combine brown sugar and eggs in medium bowl. Add flour and mix well.

- Fold in walnuts and coconut and pour over crust. Bake for 20 to 25 minutes or until set in center. Cool in pan and cut into squares. Serves 20.

TIP: *Serve these delicious squares with a scoop of ice cream for a great dessert.*

When the recipe says to "beat" the ingredients, it means to stir rapidly in a circular motion. You can do this with an electric mixer (usually set to medium speed) or by hand. One hundred strokes by hand roughly equals 1 minute by electric mixer.

Pecan Squares

2 cups flour	240 g
½ cup powdered sugar	60 g
1 cup (2 sticks) butter, cut up	230 g
1 (14 ounce) can sweetened condensed milk	400 g
2 eggs	
1 teaspoon vanilla	5 ml
1 (7 ounce) package almond-toffee bits	200 g
1 cup chopped pecans	110 g

- Preheat oven to 350° (175 C).

- Combine flour and powdered sugar in medium bowl and mix well. Cut in butter with pastry blender or fork until crumbly.

- Press mixture evenly into sprayed 9 x 13-inch (23 x 33 cm) baking pan and bake for 15 minutes.

- Combine sweetened condensed milk, eggs, vanilla, toffee bits and pecans in bowl and pour into prepared crust. Bake for 25 minutes or until golden brown.

- Cool and cut into squares. Yields 4 dozen squares.

Hello Dollies

1½ cups graham cracker crumbs	155 g
1 (6 ounce) package chocolate chips	170 g
1 cup flaked coconut	85 g
1¼ cups chopped pecans	140 g
1 (14 ounce) can sweetened condensed milk	400 g

- Preheat oven to 350° (175° C).

- Sprinkle cracker crumbs in 9 x 9-inch (23 x 23 cm) square pan. Layer chocolate chips, coconut and pecans. Pour sweetened condensed milk over top of layered ingredients.

- Bake for 25 to 30 minutes. Cool and cut into squares. Serves 20.

Rocky Road Bars

1 (12 ounce) package semi-sweet chocolate chips	340 g
1 (14 ounce) can sweetened condensed milk	400 g
2 tablespoons butter	30 g
2 cups dry-roasted peanuts	290 g
1 (10 ounce) package miniature marshmallows	280 g

- Place chocolate chips, sweetened condensed milk and butter in double boiler. Heat until chocolate and butter melt, stirring constantly.

- Remove from heat and stir in peanuts and marshmallows.

- Spread mixture quickly on wax paper-lined 9 x 13-inch (23 x 33 cm) pan. Refrigerate for at least 2 hours. Cut into bars and store in refrigerator. Serves 18.

Lemon-Angel Bars

1 (1 pound) package 1-step angel food cake mix	455 g
1 (20 ounce) can lemon pie filling	570 g
⅓ cup (⅔ stick) butter, softened	75 g
1 (16 ounce) box powdered sugar	455 g
2 tablespoons lemon juice	30 ml

- Preheat oven to 350° (175 ° C). Combine cake mix and lemon pie filling in bowl and stir to mix well.

- Pour into sprayed 9 x 13-inch (23 x 33 cm) baking pan and bake for 20 minutes or until done. Remove cake from oven just before cake is done.

- Combine butter, powdered sugar and lemon juice in bowl and spread over hot layer. Cake will sink down a little in middle, so make sure frosting is on edges of cake as well as in middle.

- When cool, cut into 18 to 24 bars and store in refrigerator. Bars can be served at room temperature or cold. Yields 18 to 24 bars.

Brownies and bars are much easier to remove from the pan if you line the pan with foil. Here's an easy method. Turn the pan upside down and cover it with a big enough piece to cover the sides as well as the bottom of the pan. Be sure to place the foil shiny side down. Press the foil around the pan, carefully remove it and turn the pan over. Fit the shaped foil, shiny side up, into the pan. Use a paper towel to smooth it down.

Fruit Fajitas

1 (20 ounce) can fruit
   pie filling   570 g
10 small flour tortillas
1½ cups sugar   300 g
¾ cup (1½ sticks) butter   170 g
1 teaspoon almond
   flavoring   5 ml

- Divide fruit equally on tortillas,
  roll and place in 9 x 13-inch
  (23 x 33 cm) baking dish.
  Combine 2 cups (500 ml) water,
  sugar and butter in saucepan and
  bring to a boil.

- Add almond flavoring and pour
  mixture over flour tortillas.
  Place in refrigerator and let soak
  1 to 24 hours.

- When ready to bake, preheat
  oven to 350° (175° C).

- Bake for 20 to 25 minutes
  until brown and bubbly.
  Serves 8 to 10.

Oreo Sundae

1 (19 ounce) package
   Oreo® cookies,
   crushed   540 g
½ cup (1 stick) butter,
   melted   115 g
½ gallon vanilla ice
   cream, softened   1.9 L
2 (12 ounce) jars fudge
   ice cream topping   2 (340 g)
1 (12 ounce) carton
   whipped topping,
   thawed   340 g
Maraschino cherries

- Set aside ½ cup (30 g) cookie
  crumbs for topping. Combine
  remaining crumbs and butter
  in bowl to form crust. Pour
  mixture into sprayed
  9 x 13-inch (23 x 33 cm)
  pan and press down.

- Spread softened ice cream over
  crust and add layer of fudge
  sauce. Top with whipped
  topping and reserved crumbs.
  Garnish with cherries and freeze
  until ready to serve. Serves 12.

Lemon Lush

1¼ cups flour   150 g
⅔ cup (⅓ stick) butter 150 g
½ cup chopped pecans 55 g
1 cup powdered sugar 120 g
1 (8 ounce) package
    cream cheese,
    softened   230 g
1 (12 ounce) carton
    whipped topping,
    thawed, divided 340 g
2 (3.4 ounce)
    packages instant
    lemon pudding   2 (100 g)
1 tablespoon lemon
    juice   15 ml
2¾ cups milk   425 g

- Preheat oven to 375° (175° C).

- Combine flour, butter and pecans in bowl and pat down into 9 x 13-inch (23 x 33 cm) baking dish. Bake for 15 minutes.

- Beat powdered sugar and cream cheese in bowl until fluffy and fold in 2 cups (150 g) whipped topping. Spread mixture over nut crust.

- In separate bowl, combine pudding, lemon juice and milk and beat. Spread over second layer. Top with remaining whipped topping and refrigerate. To serve, cut into squares. Serves 20.

Baked Apples

4 - 5 large baking apples
1 tablespoon lemon juice   15 ml
⅓ cup Craisins®   40 g
½ cup chopped pecans   55 g
**¾ cup packed brown
    sugar   165 g**
**½ teaspoon ground
    cinnamon   2 ml**
**¼ cup (½ stick) butter,
    melted   60 g**
Caramel ice cream topping

- Scoop out center of each apple and leave cavity about ½ inch (1.2 cm) from bottom.

- Peel top of apples down about 1 inch (2.5 cm) and brush lemon juice on peeled edges.

- Combine Craisins®, pecans, brown sugar, cinnamon and butter in bowl. Spoon mixture into apple cavities.

- Pour ½ cup (125 ml) water in oval slow cooker and place apples on bottom.

- Cover and cook on LOW for 1 to 3 hours or until tender.

- Serve warm or room temperature drizzled with caramel ice cream topping. Serves 5.

How many times during our childhoods did we hear the adage, "An apple a day keeps the doctor away." As it turns out, the truth is the apple is a very nutritious food. Apples contain vitamin C plus many other antioxidants, which are cancer fighters.

Creamy Banana Pudding

This is a quick and easy way to make the old favorite banana pudding.

1 (14 ounce) can sweetened
    condensed milk   **400 g**
1 (3.4 ounce) package
    instant vanilla
    pudding mix   **100 g**
1 (8 ounce) carton
    whipped topping,
    thawed   **230 g**
36 vanilla wafers
3 bananas

- Combine sweetened condensed milk and 1½ cups (375 ml) cold water in large bowl.

- Add pudding mix and beat well.

- Refrigerate for 5 minutes and fold in whipped topping.

- Spoon 1 cup (250 ml) pudding mixture into 3-quart (3 L) glass serving bowl. Top with wafers, bananas and pudding. Repeat layers twice and end with pudding.

- Cover and refrigerate. Serves 8 to 10.

Sweetened condensed milk has 50% of the water removed. The remaining mixture is 40% sugar and is very sticky and sweet.

Index

365 Easy One-Dish Recipes

for Everyday Family Meals

Cookbooks Published by
Cookbook Resources, LLC
Bringing Family and Friends to the Table

*The Best of Cooking
with 3 Ingredients*

*The Ultimate Cooking
with 4 Ingredients*

*Easy Cooking
with 5 Ingredients*

*Healthy Cooking
with 4 Ingredients*

*Gourmet Cooking
with 5 Ingredients*

*4-Ingredient Recipes
for 30-Minute Meals*

*Essential 3-4-5
Ingredient Recipes*

The Best 1001 Short, Easy Recipes

1001 Fast Easy Recipes

1001 Community Recipes

*Busy Woman's
Quick & Easy Recipes*

*Busy Woman's
Slow Cooker Recipes*

Easy Slow Cooker Cookbook

Easy One-Dish Meals

Easy Potluck Recipes

Easy Casseroles

Easy Desserts

Sunday Night Suppers

Easy Church Suppers

365 Easy Meals

365 Easy Chicken Recipes

365 Easy Soups and Stews

365 Easy Vegetarian Recipes

Quick Fixes with Cake Mixes

*Kitchen Keepsakes/
More Kitchen Keepsakes*

Gifts for the Cookie Jar

*All New Gifts
for the Cookie Jar*

Muffins In A Jar

The Big Bake Sale Cookbook

*Classic Tex-Mex
and Texas Cooking*

Classic Southwest Cooking

Miss Sadie's Southern Cooking

Texas Longhorn Cookbook

Cookbook 25 Years

A Little Taste of Texas

A Little Taste of Texas II

*Trophy Hunters'
Wild Game Cookbook*

Recipe Keeper

*Leaving Home Cookbook
and Survival Guide*

*Classic Pennsylvania
Dutch Cooking*

Easy Diabetic Recipes

**cookbook
resources** ® LLC

www.cookbookresources.com

Your Ultimate Source for Easy Cookbooks